A Place Apart

Hebden Bridge

*as seen through the eyes of
the Spencer family
in the late nineteenth century*

CHRISTOPHER COLLIER

The Choir Press

Copyright © 2024 Christopher Collier

All rights reserved. No part of this publication may be reproduced or transmitted in any form or by any means, electronic or mechanical including photocopying, recording or any information storage or retrieval system, without prior permission in writing from the publishers.

The right of Christopher Collier to be identified as the author of this work has been asserted by him in accordance with the Copyright, Designs and Patents Act 1988

First published in the United Kingdom in 2024 by
The Choir Press

ISBN 978-1-78963-379-5

Cover painting: Hebden Bridge, from Palace House, Fairfield, by John Holland, 1869, courtesy of Calderdale Museums and Bridgeman Images.

Contents

Preface	vii
Introduction	1

1.	The Pennine Weaver	6
2.	Fustianopolis	10
3.	Cathedrals of Nonconformity	16
4.	Growing Up	21
5.	The Waltons of Foster Mill	28
6.	Connections	34
7.	Setting Up Shop	38
8.	Taking the Train	42
9.	Putting Down Roots	45
10.	Know Your Greenwoods	49
11.	Cottonopolis	52
12.	Game Changers	58
13.	All the News	62
14.	Epidemic	65
15.	Home Affairs	70
16.	Chapel and Choir	78
17.	Good Works	82
18.	Relaxing	88
19.	The Wider World	92
20.	Moving House	97
21.	From Township to Town	104
22.	The Spencer Children	111
23.	An Abrupt Departure	121
24.	Family Scandal	124

25. Taking Refuge	127
26. Hard Times	132
27. Afterlife	137
Appendix One	140
Appendix Two	142
Appendix Three	144
Appendix Four	145
Acknowledgements	147
Notes	149
Bibliography	158

A section of the map of Yorkshire in Pigot's County Atlas of England, published in 1840. Both the Rochdale Canal and the newly opened Manchester and Leeds Railway follow the valley of the river Calder. The map could not have been more up to date: the Manchester to Littleborough section of the M&LR opened in July 1839, Hebden Bridge to Normanton (near Wakefield) in October 1840, and the section in between, Littleborough to Hebden Bridge via the Summit Tunnel, in March 1841. To locate Hebden Bridge, find the point just below Heptonstall and Old Town where the Haworth road meets the railway, road and canal.

'This book offers a vivid account of the life of a small entrepreneur in a textile town providing an insight into the lives of those who rarely receive the attention of historians.'

Alan Fowler, formerly Principal Lecturer of Economic and Social History, Manchester Metropolitan University

'I have read your book with interest and enjoyment. Beyond the details of your family the research contributes to our understanding of several important issues in nineteenth- and early twentieth-century British history. A sensitive appreciation of the diversity and complexity of industrial and cultural change is vital and this study offers much.'

David Howell, Professor of Politics, University of York

'Brilliant piece of writing. Once I started reading, I couldn't put it down. A really interesting story told in great detail and with passion and pride.'

Michael Peel, local Hebden Bridge historian

Preface

From handlooms on the hills to mills lining the valleys – that was the Pennine story in the nineteenth century. Hebden Bridge was no different, but it came late to the party, and despite its Yorkshire affiliation it looked over the border into Lancashire and down to Manchester to make its fortune.

Sheltering below the moors, at a junction of two rivers, and with 'top and bottom' houses climbing the hillside, it looked to be – and it was – a place apart.

This was Joseph Spencer's world, in which as a young man with ambition and good contacts he built a successful business as a tailor and outfitter. The growth of his business mirrored the rise of the town. So too the lives of his family. They grew up in a Nonconformist landscape and at the same time experienced all the excitement of a period of extraordinary change. This was the Victorian heyday, the decades that made Hebden Bridge as they made the family.

The family left the town in 1901. It was an abrupt departure, to avoid scandal when Joseph and Emily discovered that their daughter, Lilian, was pregnant by a local boy. That is a story in itself.

Joseph maintained links with the town until 1903. Thereafter he focused on the Manchester side of the business, leaving his eldest son, my grandfather, Thomas Spencer (born 1878), to run the Hebden Bridge shop. The business ran into financial trouble in 1907. The various premises, in several Lancashire towns as well as Hebden Bridge, were sold off.

Reliving the period, town and family, has been an extraordinary experience, something of which I hope is conveyed in these pages. In a number of places I've had to make assumptions, on the evidence available, which may be open to challenge. A diarist or two, a Hebden Bridge Kilvert, would have been useful. Letters also, had the Spencers been a letter-writing family. But the newspapers of the time have provided a marvellous if somewhat random substitute.

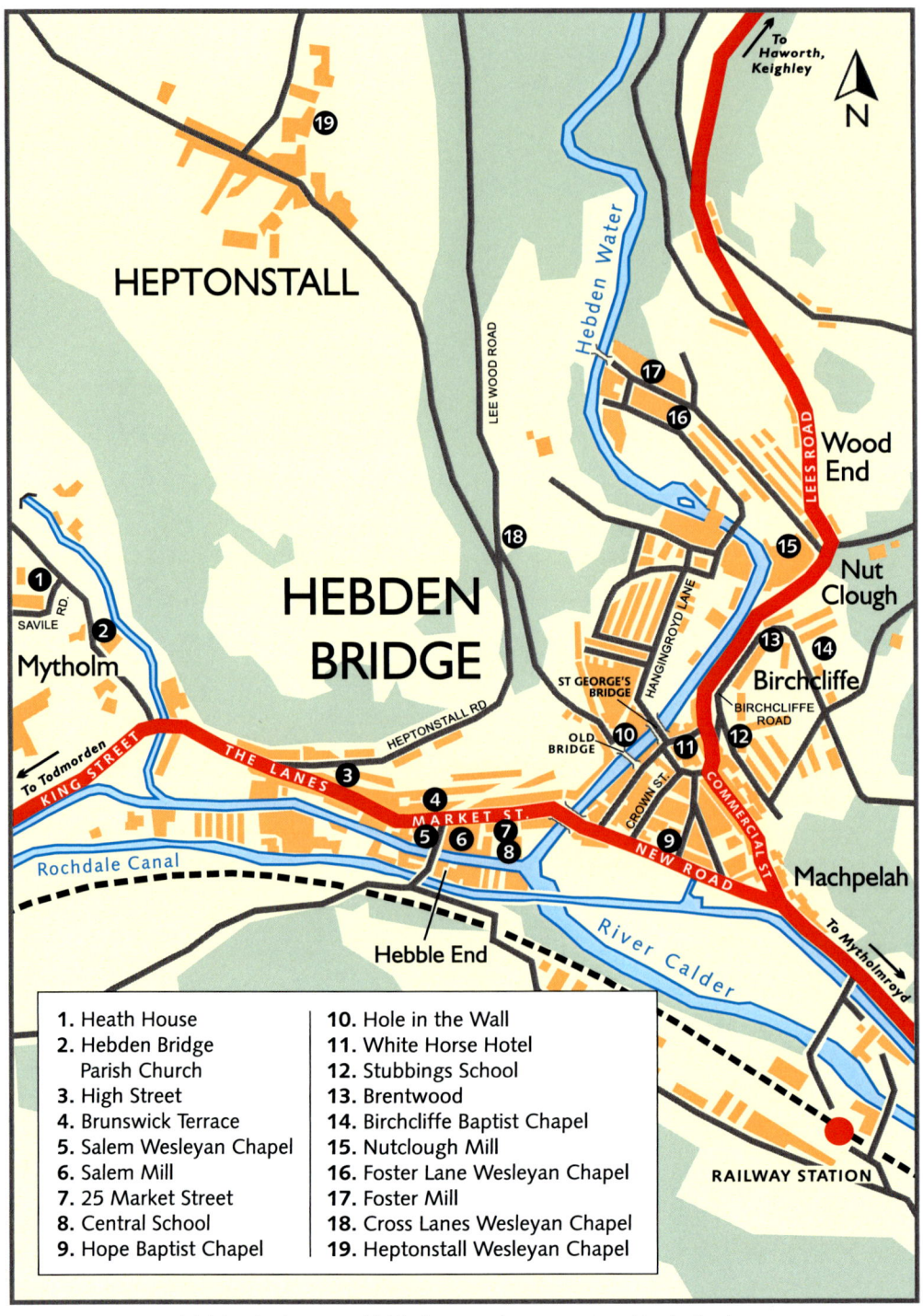

Hebden Bridge, circa 1900, showing places mentioned in the book.

Introduction

The thirty years from 1871 to 1901 during which Joseph served his apprenticeship and built a successful business in Hebden Bridge were a period of extraordinary change. Towns took in swathes of countryside, with mill and housing planted cheek by jowl. Where handloom weavers had been tied to their cottages their offspring walked short distances to the mills along, if they were lucky, streets recently laid with setts.

Hebden Bridge exemplified that transformation. The demand for clothing made from fustian, a hard-wearing form of corduroy, with destinations in the UK and further afield, helped create a landscape not only of new and ever-bigger mills, but also a new town where before there had been no more than a village. The town prospered, gained an identity, and a civic pride.

The twentieth century may have brought strikes and declining demand, but that doesn't change the reality that there was great energy and optimism about Hebden Bridge in the years Joseph worked there. Change back then was normal – change at an almost exponential rate. It could have been chaos, but instead business and managerial skills came together in a quite remarkable way. 'What was new was the desire, and ability, to impose a rational order upon the relations created by the new productive system.'[1] If you were lucky to be there at the right time, as Joseph was, and you showed initiative, and you had contacts (and they always help), then the world was an exciting place to be.

The poet Ted Hughes grew up in Mytholmroyd, a mile down the road from Hebden Bridge, at another tipping point. The mills were closing and often left as relics in the landscape. 'The sunk mill-towns were cemeteries.'[2] Romance lies in the rocks and the winds and the dereliction. Romantic it may be, but it is false trail.

It hides the lived reality and the vitality of Hebden Bridge as it was in the late nineteenth century. And it could not be more misleading regarding the town as it is today. Past and present come together to extraordinary effect. It is, as it was then, a place apart.

It is also, then and now, a contradiction. It has always been a Yorkshire town but, as far at least as its manufacturing economy was concerned, the road and rail routes over the Pennines to Lancashire were a more natural direction of travel than down the Calder to Halifax. Unlike its Yorkshire neighbours, with their focus on wool, Hebden Bridge during the nineteenth century came to specialise in cotton spinning, and then weaving, and in cotton products, and specifically fustian.

'Always a Yorkshire town' – but its status as a town came late, as we will see. Likewise its name. Trains in the early days would have been passing through a landscape where communities were denominated by township names dating back to medieval times. They are the names that appear in the early census records. Several ancient townships met in what became Hebden Bridge, with their borders generally along rivers. Hebden Bridge as it is today was mostly in Wadsworth and Heptonstall townships. Across the river Calder lay Erringden, and to the west Stansfield. The Spencers who spent most of their lives in Heptonstall township may have only on rare occasions set foot in Heptonstall village on the hill above.[3]

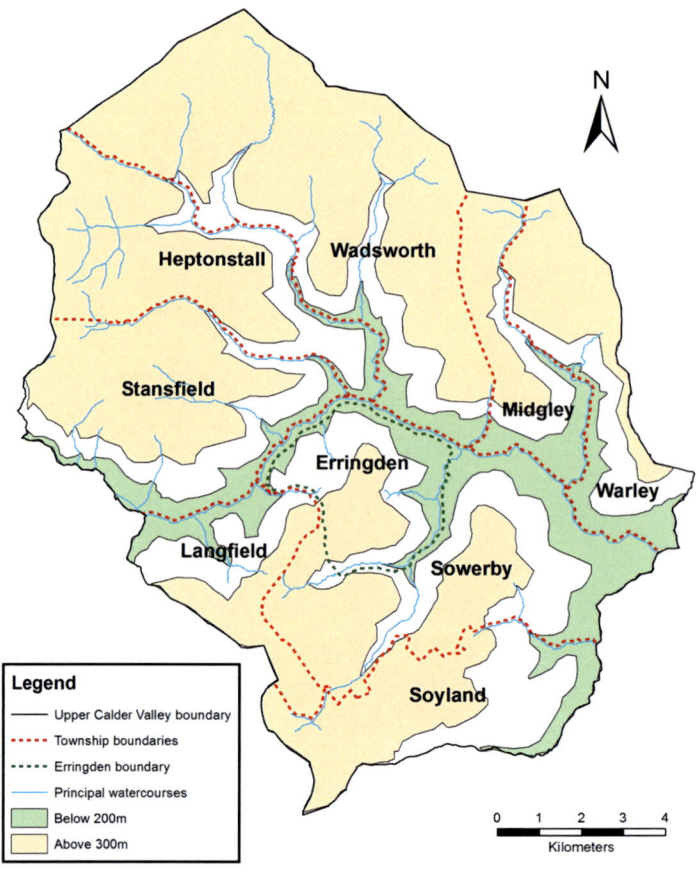

The townships of the Upper Calder Valley as they were from medieval times. What became the town of Hebden Bridge grew up around the junction of the three rivers, Calder, Hebden and Colden, in the centre of the map. Cross Vale is the valley to the south. (Reproduced from Nigel Smith, The Medieval Park of Erringden, Hebden Bridge Local History Society, 2021)

The Spencer family

The year 1871 is the first time Joseph appears in the records as a working man. He was sixteen, and his profession is already listed as a tailor, and not fustian cutter, the occupation of so many young men of his time.

Joseph's grandfather was Zechariah, a shopkeeper, who married Ginney Cockcroft in 1810. They never, it seems, moved far from High Street, which lay to the north of Bridge Lanes in the tight angle with Heptonstall Road. This had been one of the earliest areas of settlement in the town, dating to the early nineteenth century. Back-to-back terraces climbed steeply, with internal stairs giving access to dwellings at several levels. The area lay in stark contrast to the surrounding fields, which continued to be open until Market Street was developed after 1870. High Street was demolished in the 1960s.[4]

Their son, Thomas, married Mary Rushton in 1840. He was at that time a cordwainer (shoemaker). Thomas and Mary had five children: Jane, Hannah, James, Joseph and Mary Ellen. Joseph was born in 1854, at an address on High Street.[5]

The 1851 census provided information on a range of household occupations which were typical of the time. Thomas had become a fustian cutter. The Spencers and the dwellings adjacent to them on High Street were listed as follows:

Firth (mother and son): pauper and coat seller
Spencer (husband and wife): a fustian cutter and a winder (cotton)
Greenwoods: a pin seller, a stretcher (silk), and an umbrella coverer
Inghams: woolcombers.

Bridge Lanes, c.1900, at the junction with Heptonstall Road. High Street lay behind the tenements which follow the line of Bridge Lanes toward the town. The smart attire suggests the walkers were heading to an event at one of the chapels. (PHDA-ALC00549)

The Walton family

Emily Walton, Joseph's wife-to-be, is listed in the 1871 census as a cotton winder. She would have been fourteen. Her father, Thomas Walton, was born in 1821, her mother, Sarah Hodgson, in 1820. Thomas and Sarah were married in 1843. There is no father shown in the marriage register, which implies that Thomas was illegitimate.[6] The family were Wesleyan Methodists*, and the marriage may have been at the Wesleyan Chapel in Heptonstall.

Thomas is listed in the 1861 and 1871 censuses as living at 1 Foster Mill. In the 1861 census he is described as 'manager of cotton mill', and 1871 census as 'manager and manufacturer'. Thomas and Sarah Walton had five children: Elizabeth Ann, Sarah Grace, Emily, Robert Spence and Mary Louisa. Emily was born in 1855 at Foster Mill House.

Hebden Bridge

Joseph was an apprentice tailor, Emily a cotton winder in 1871. The opportunity was there, as Hebden Bridge opened up to the world, for anyone with ability and initiative to make their mark.

They were faced with a working world where hours were long, but greatly reduced from early century levels, with the introduction in 1847 of the ten-hour day for women and young people. The working day was (from 1850) fixed as 6 a.m. to 6 p.m. in summer, 7 a.m. to 7 p.m. in winter. The 1860s saw provisions which had applied only to textile mills extended to include other textile trades, including bleaching and dyeing, and fustian cutting. The biggest development was the move to the 'half-day Saturday', campaigns for which had been building since the 1850s, and the recreational and sporting activities it made possible, from the 1880s onwards.†

The thirty years to 1901, when the family left Hebden Bridge, saw the country, and Hebden Bridge with it, change in a quite extraordinary way. The UK's population grew from 27 million in 1851 to 45 million in 1913, and the demand for working-men's clothing grew with it. 'Artisanal apparel' was Hebden Bridge's almost exclusive focus. Taking the coal industry as a prime

---

* Wesleyan Methodist Connexion was the name given to the mainstream Methodist movement in England, 'connexion' being changed to 'church' in 1891. Not until the several strands of Methodism came together in 1932 did the name 'Methodist Church' become established. Salem, in Hebden Bridge, and Heptonstall were known as Wesleyan not Methodist chapels and that's how I've described them throughout.
† It is no accident that the Football League began life in 1888, at a time when Saturday afternoons were opening up new opportunities for both players and spectators. Six of the twelve teams in the new league were from Lancashire towns. (Burnley, one of the twelve, was an easy train ride from Hebden Bridge.)

example, in 1851 there were 216,000 miners, and by 1891 it had increased to 517,000. 'The factories of Hebden Bridge were making corduroy trousers by the thousands for the miners.'[7]

But, as we will see, this wasn't the market Joseph Spencer catered to. He wasn't supplying big contracts. His aspiration was to be a tailor, to move away from wholesale, ready-made clothing to tailored, bespoke attire for a newly prosperous working-class population, with surplus income and time and, alongside, an aspirant managerial middle class. He opened branches in other towns, all Lancashire cotton towns, with, it seems, this market in mind. 'The newest things in Worsted Coatings, Suitings and Trouserings' ran one of his advertisements.

1
The Pennine Weaver

'Scarcity promotes industry'

For an insight into the world that the Spencers and Waltons were born into there is no better guide than E. P. Thompson's *The Making of the English Working Class*.[1] Many historians, most recently Robert Tombs, in *The English and their History*[2], take a rosier view of events. Thompson might agree with them to the extent that (in his words) 'over the period 1790–1840 there was a slight improvement in average material standards'. But he follows with the qualification that 'over the same period there was intensified exploitation, greater insecurity, and increasing human misery'.*

The early years of the Industrial Revolution changed the Pennine landscape in every sense.

The Pennine weaving industry had long been a cottage industry. 'In the Yorkshire domestic industry of the eighteenth century, the wool was the property, not of the weaver but of the little master-clothier. Most workers were journeymen, working for a single clothier ... In the Halifax and Leeds districts, nearly all the processes of cloth manufacture took place within a single domestic unit.'

Thompson also focuses on the weavers' pride and cultural attainments. 'Every weaving district had its weaver-poets, mathematicians, biologists, musicians, geologists ...'

The soaring output of machine yarn in the late eighteenth century lay at the heart of an 'essential loss of status'. This was a golden age when the supply of yarn and market demand fed into an extraordinary increase in the number of weavers. When demand fell away, 'reduced to complete dependence of the spinning-mill or the "putters-out" who took yarn up into the uplands, the weavers were now exposed to round after round of wage reductions'.

---

* In recent times some of the heat has gone out of the debate over the condition of the working class in Victorian times. One of Thompson's targets was the more benign position taken by the economic historian, J. L. Clapham. A comment on the History of Economic Thought website is a reminder that the old rancour hasn't quite gone away: 'Contrary to romantic anti-industrial rhetoric, (Clapham) asserted that wages and standards of living for most of the English urban working class (save for the handloom weavers) had risen significantly through the period.' Thompson would surely have countered that where the baseline was so low, talk of increases in wages and living standards could be seriously misleading.

'Scarcity promotes industry' was the watchword. Memories of a past prosperity provoked alarm: one magistrate in 1818 remembered a time 'some years ago' when weavers were 'so extravagantly paid' that they could relax in alehouses and around tea-tables.

As for trade unions, the Combination Acts of 1799 and 1800 had made them illegal, but the period to 1824, when the Acts were repealed, was paradoxically a period when 'trade unionism registered great advances'. But not amongst the weavers. The period saw both a progressive reduction in wages and a not unrelated 'breakdown of both custom and trade union protection'.

The widespread introduction of the power loom radically worsened the situation. In cotton alone there were 100,000 fewer weavers in 1840 than 1830. The legendary John Fielden, mill owner and MP for Todmorden, strongly argued the case for a minimum wage in the 1830s but to no avail. In Thompson's words, 'the condition of most weavers from the 1820s to the 1840s and beyond is commonly referred to as "indescribable"'.

It was also characterised by many historians, with whom Thompson takes issue, as 'inevitable'. Not so, in his view. 'Weavers, who wove cloth when they themselves were in rags, were forcibly educated in the vitiating error of the orthodox political economy.'

'Jack-o-Bog Eggs, Wadsworth, the last handloom weaver in the Calderdale area.'
(PHDA-ALC00786)

'It was in the weaving districts surrounding such centres as Bradford, Keighley, Halifax, Huddersfield, Todmorden, Rochdale, Bolton, Macclesfield, that the largest proportion of utterly depressed outworkers was to be found.' The *History of Typhus in Heptonstall Slack*, published in 1844, told a terrible story. 'One open stream, polluted by a slaughter-house, was in summer "a nursery of loathsome animal life".' Recounting the epidemic, Thompson plays on our emotions, but it is still a terrible story of deprivation and pollution.

The Poor Law Amendment Act

It might have been worse. The Poor Law Amendment Act of 1834 took away out-relief, 'the standby of many communities'. A Bolton weaver recorded in 1834 'very shortly I shall be under its dreadful operation. I have not merited these things …' But Todmorden was one of a number of districts which held out against its implementation. John Fielden, mill owner of Todmorden, flatly defied the law. 'Resistance was violent, protracted and intense.'

It was, as a resolution out of a public meeting in Todmorden in 1838 demonstrated, not just the harshness of the new Poor Law they opposed but also the need to defend 'that self-government which we have had handed down to us by our forefathers'. The new workhouse of the Halifax Union down the valley opened in 1841, but the six townships including Heptonstall, Stansfield and Wadsworth, out of which Hebden Bridge emerged, held on to their old workhouses until the 1870s. The rather grand Todmorden workhouse, built on a site at Lee Bottom, near Mankinholes, covered the whole area and finally opened in 1878. The building was demolished in 1996.

The story illustrates how the upper reaches of the Calder Valley really were a place apart, beyond the reach, despite the use of troops and the courts, of the Poor Law Commissioners. Whether it's true that 'in the long run the "Union workhouse" was resisted more because it symbolised the victory of central bureaucracy over local independence than because of tenderness to the poor' is surely debatable.[3] It would depend on who you talked to. But taken together they saw off the new Poor Law for more than forty years.

Joseph Greenwood

Andrew Bibby in his book, *All Our Own Work: The co-operative pioneers of Hebden Bridge and their mill*, quotes from the memoirs of the mill's legendary co-founder and manager, Joseph Greenwood. For his family the handloom was the only work available. It was irregular and poorly paid: 'We had oatmeal porridge and skim-milk for food with rarely a change during the week.' But handlooms were disappearing. In Greenwood's words, 'The same windows that used to be lighted after dark from within are now in darkness.'[4]

Greenwood grew up in Stephenson House, on a hillside above nearby Mytholmroyd, but his experience, as recounted by Bibby, may have been similar to that of Joseph Spencer's parents living on High Street, Hebden Bridge. Greenwood's contribution to the household as a very young child was bobbin-winding, but the opportunity came his way, at the age of nine, to learn the craft of fustian cutting 'when a newly married couple moved into the house next door. The man made clogs: his wife and young Joseph worked at the fustian frames.' Six years later, in 1849, he left home to work for John Moss of Machpelah, described as a fustian manufacturer and linen-draper.

Joseph's future would be linked by marriage to the Spencer family: his eldest son, Virgil, was to marry Joseph Spencer's sister, Mary Ellen.

2

Fustianopolis

The question usually asked is – what is fustian? It is best known in the form of corduroy and moleskin. In the case of corduroy, which is of its nature hard-wearing, cloth woven on the loom required an additional and highly skilled process known as fustian cutting. This involved cutting the raised loops created in the weft during the weaving process 'using a specialised knife to create the characteristic pile or ribbed surface'.[1] The cutter slid the knife along the raised edge, a process he would repeat several hundred times a day.[2] It remained a hand process until the early twentieth century and could be carried on as readily in the home as in the factory.

A fustian cutter, c.1890. This photograph indicates both the precision and the monotony of the fustian cutter's work. See page 50 for a report of an accident in 1878 to Joseph Greenwood's son, Virgil, at Nutclough Mill. (PHDA-HLS06075)

Manchester had been an early centre for fustians. One reason why its manufacture came to the Upper Calder Valley was the quality of the local water, from a multitude of hillside springs, soft by reason of the local Millstone Grit rock, and thereby well suited to dyeing and finishing cloth. Fustian, tight-woven and hard-wearing, became the standard workwear for the miners and navvies, the dockworkers and steelworkers, who put in the hard and brutal labour behind the extraordinary expansion of British industry in the later nineteenth century. Other towns also expanded their manufacture of fustians but it was Hebden Bridge that achieved a pre-eminence which earned it the name 'Fustianopolis'.

Early years

Fustian's status could not have been foreseen in the earlier decades of the century. In the words of Sam Moore, writing in 1913, 'earlier in the 19th century the most important development was the building of large spinning mills ... Several of the firms were manufacturers as well as spinners ... At a later period weaving was enabled more, and spinning began to decline.'[3]

This followed a pattern seen across Lancashire, underlining the links between this corner of West Yorkshire, and specifically Todmorden and Hebden Bridge, and its county neighbour. 'New specialised spinning mills were built by large limited companies in south-east Lancashire whilst in north-east Lancashire a multitude of weaving firms were formed by private entrepreneurs.'[4] (Hebden Bridge's neighbour, Todmorden, had the status of a border town, with one half in each county.)

The 1851 census records 1,600 people working in the cotton mills. Only sixty-five were working in fustians.[5] Among them was Thomas, Joseph Spencer's father, one of forty-seven described as 'fustian cutters'. There were 'several hundreds still engaged in handloom weaving', and they are another reason why fustian manufacture took hold in the area. Fustian cutting was a hand process, and handloom weavers who resisted mill work could turn instead to fustian cutting.

In 1862 the Relief Committee set up to alleviate distress caused by the disruption of the supply of cotton during the American Civil War estimated there were almost four thousand people employed in the mills in the wider area. With mills and workforce already in place it meant the switch to weaving fustian cloth could be readily accommodated. Mills such as the Nutclough Co-operative would in time take the process of cutting itself in-house.

The local trade

By mid-century, fustian manufacturers were 'doing business in a small way'. (Sam Moore) 'The sales were made direct to country tailors in ends or short lengths.'

'About the beginning of this time [after 1865] the fustian merchants who travelled the countryside found a demand for fustian garments instead of fustian pieces. This led one of them to start making garments, others followed and were apparently successful, and in short time quite a number of firms were engaged in making ready-made fustian clothing.'

Sam Moore makes the point that this applied 'only to the local trade, for by this time a considerable amount of "Manchester trade" was being done:

that is, pieces were "cut" on commission in larger quantities, and carried to and from the station ...' It was no accident that one of the earliest railways out of Manchester was the Lancashire and Yorkshire Railway, connecting Manchester and Leeds, Leeds being the great centre of the garment industry. Hebden Bridge had an excellent train connection at a very early stage.

But it is this 'local trade' on which we need to focus. It was, as Sam Moore goes on to emphasise, the local manufacturers' direct and close links with the actual consumer that led to the development of the ready-made trade.

'The first wholesale clothier'

The 'one of them' referred to by Sam Moore is usually thought to have been William Barker. He is reputed to have been the first wholesale clothier in Hebden Bridge. By 'wholesale clothier' this usually meant producing ready-made clothing for the wholesale market. His fustian cutting and dyeing business is recorded in the 1861 census, but not yet as a clothier. The next forty years saw a rapid expansion and in a leaflet from 1900 the business claimed to have been 'established half a century', as 'Fustian Manufacturers, Bleacher, Dyer and Finisher and Wholesale Clothier'.*

As Michael Peel points out there were other candidates for the title of first wholesale clothier. (One was John Kershaw, another John Crowther, of whom more later.) But none built up to any kind of scale. From manufacturer to wholesale clothier, in time Barker's company covered every activity.

The sewing machine, as patented by Isaac Merritt Singer in the USA in 1851, had been the game changer. Barker records that his wife Peggy and their two daughters at an early stage 'began making garments, sewing them by hand'.[6] 'They soon introduced sewing machines, although at first these could only be used for sewing straight seams and all the finishing had to be done by hand.'[7]

In the 1861 census, Joseph Spencer's elder sisters by more than ten years, Jane and Hannah, are both listed as tending sewing machines. It's possible, though I've no direct evidence for this, that Jane and Hannah, and maybe their father as well, were working for William Barker.

Working at scale came several years later. Michael Peel quotes a later claim by one of Barker's employees that that he 'mechanised the sewing machines at Barker's factory at Wood Top' at some point between 1865 and 1872. This suggests that only then did his activities as a clothier really take off.

---

* For this section I'm indebted to two unpublished articles, under the title 'Early Clothiers', by local Hebden Bridge historian, Michael Peel.

Benjamin Smith, who had at one stage worked for William Barker, was also active as a clothier at an early stage. He had a party on New Year's Day 1866 attended by forty of his 'seamsters' and 'seamistresses'. (This last term a neologism which rather sadly hasn't stood the test of time.) *White's Directory* for that year lists Benjamin Smith as Hebden Bridge's only wholesale clothier.

Smith's business was short-lived and taken over by J. P. Holmes who 'ran a shop selling ready-made clothing at a substantial discount … He named his shop the "Working Man's Clothing Depot"'. But by 1871 he'd moved over the border into Lancashire, to Bacup.*

Colin Spencer in his *History of Hebden Bridge* describes the processes involved, drawing on the 1871 census returns, as they related to William Barker. 'First of all the cloth was cut to a pattern and the census lists a "master cutter and tailor", born in Manchester, and a "tailor cutter-out". The cloth, cut to size, was passed to a machinist and there were about twenty women described as "machinist" or "sewing machinist", or, in one case, "machinist of boys' cotton suits".'

From this point the demand for cloth grew at extraordinary speed. New mills, such as the Fustian Co-operative at Nutclough, were established, and existing mills expanded into weaving to meet the demand for cloth, and into manufacturing to produce the finished garments.

Kelly's Directory for 1867 lists nine fustian manufacturers in Hebden Bridge, including William Barker, with virtually none in the neighbouring townships. In 1877 it lists thirteen fustian manufacturers, including the Moss brothers who, just seven years later, were to sell the land to Joseph Spencer on which he then built his shop. Four wholesale clothiers are listed.[8] In 1893 there are seventeen fustian manufacturers and in 1897 twenty-six.

Mills in the landscape

Businesses connected to the fustian trade may have proliferated but big mills still dominated the landscape. Foster, Hangingroyd, Bridge and Nutclough Mills lay adjacent to Hebden Water as it descended the valley. Salem and Calder Mills sat four-square next to the canal and the river Calder itself. They had long histories, with cotton spinning the focus earlier in the century. But all of them in time adapted to a changing world.[9]

---

* Workwear may not, as we will see, have been Joseph Spencer's primary market but an advertisement from 1887 'calls special attention to his fustian clothing'. He was supplying lamplighters' suits to the council in the 1890s.

Old Bridge and Hebden Water, with the chimney of Bridge Mill beyond, c.1880. (PHDA-ALC00504)

Bridge Mill had by the 1890s passed into the hands of Greenwood and Pickles, who produced ready-made clothing there until the 1950s.

Hangingroyd had been converted to fustian manufacture at an early stage. 'In 1871 a new dye works, weaving shed, engine and boiler house were added.'

Nutclough had been a cotton mill before being bought by the Hebden Bridge Fustian Manufacturing Co-operative Society in 1873. It was on garment-making that they built their fortune.

Foster had been a cotton mill before the big fire, of which more below, in 1888. The rebuilt mill focused on the manufacture of ready-made garments.

Further up the valley lay two Midgehole mills which were bought by a Salford firm of dyers in 1861, bringing with them dye workers and fustian cutters from Manchester. Gibson Mill was used for fustian manufacture until the 1890s, after which it took on the role it still enjoys today looking after the multitude of visitors to Hardcastle Crags.

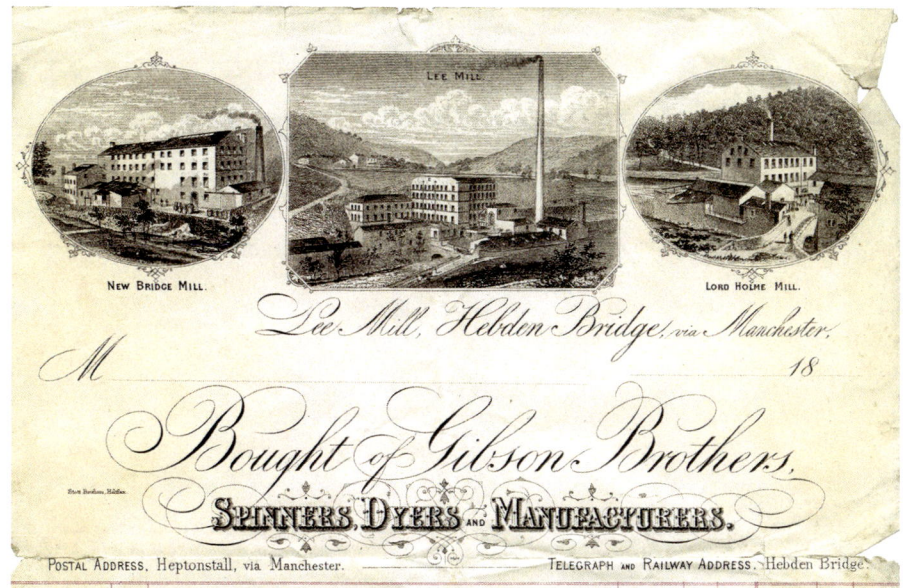

A billhead for New Bridge, Lee and Lord Holme (also known as Gibson) Mills. Note both Hebden Bridge and Heptonstall are described as 'via Manchester': old county loyalties counted for little when high commerce was involved. (Hebden Bridge Local History Society Archive, Gibson Collection)

The tight confines of the valley restricted further development and allowed the town to develop its own highly distinctive identity, looking across the Pennines to Lancashire rather than to the mill landscapes further down the Calder.

By the time Joseph sold his business in Hebden Bridge in 1907 there had been further changes. Fustian cutting, for so long a hand process, had been fully mechanised. It was in dyeing and finishing, where Hebden Bridge had an established advantage, that the town led the country in the years before 1914. Cloth was brought in from other fustian manufacturing towns over in Lancashire for dyeing and finishing to meet the surging demand for ready-made clothing.

3
Cathedrals of Nonconformity

The Spencers and Waltons were Wesleyan Methodists, in a territory which had been split by various evangelical revivals over the previous 100 years into multiple denominations. There is evidence that Heptonstall Chapel had long been the fulcrum of the Waltons' social and spiritual life. (See page 4) The allegiance of Joseph's parents is less clear, though his betrothal to Emily Walton is likely to have come about through a chapel connection.

To a degree that's difficult to comprehend today, the religious landscape was as real as the physical and industrial landscapes, and like any landscape it had its fractures. Its physical manifestation lay in the number of chapels which marked the hillsides. The Church of England could almost be discounted. The high Pennines had long been the territory of the weavers not the landed gentry. For weavers read mill workers – little changed as the century progressed.

Passion lay with the Nonconformists, and they divided between Methodists, themselves divided between mainstream Wesleyan and breakaways, including Primitives and Independents, and Baptists, who might be Strict (also known as Particular) or General depending on attitudes to baptism and the grace and generosity of God. (In Hebden Bridge, the Birchcliffe Chapel Baptists were General, and the Hope Particular.) Wesleyans had a more relaxed attitude to the working of God's grace than the Baptists. Wesleyans welcomed infants into the church at baptism, Baptists insisted it must be an adult decision.

The number of chapels which still dot the Pennine landscape testify to the passion of the early preachers. While allegiances could be fickle enthusiasm ran deep, and invaded social as well as spiritual life. But, by the late nineteenth century, if you were born a Wesleyan or Baptist of one stripe or another you were likely to stay that way.

It was also a moral landscape. Among working-class communities the stigma of illegitimacy could be overcome: Emily's father and Joseph's eldest sister were both born out of wedlock. But as Wesleyan Methodists achieved new levels of prosperity and, with it, status, middle-class values came to underpin their theology. A sterner Nonconformity infiltrated the built landscape, and that included strictures relating to marriage. This would have great significance for the Spencer family.

Competition

The first chapel on the Salem site in Hebden Bridge had opened in 1824. (It was in that chapel fifty-three years later that Joseph and Emily Spencer were married.) It had originally been part of the Todmorden circuit, and 'the best attended chapel not only in the town but in the circuit'. Nearby, Cross Lanes Chapel, built 'largely by the efforts of Salem members', opened in 1840.[1]

Salem Wesleyan Chapel, opened 1824, demolished 1885. Its design has more in common with a mill or warehouse than a place of worship. (Reproduced from E. R. Dickenson, History of Salem Chapel)

In March 1851 a religious census recorded that 'Salem had a morning congregation of 204, with 261 children in the Sunday School, and an evening congregation of 465'.[2] A new Hebden Bridge circuit was formed in 1862, with Salem as the lead chapel. A new Sunday school building opened in 1874, and a new and grander chapel in 1885, of which more later.

The first Baptist chapel (of the General persuasion) on the Birchcliffe site opened in 1764. A new chapel replaced the old in 1833, and a third chapel, on a site lower down the hill, opened in 1899 (now the Birchcliffe Centre). The Particular Baptists' home after 1777 was the Ebenezer Chapel (now the Hebden Bridge Arts Centre) until in 1858 it was replaced by a new chapel, known as Hope Chapel, in what became the centre of town.[3]

Only in 1832, consecrated in 1833, did Hebden Bridge get a parish church (St James the Great), some way out of town[4], and even then its status was that of a 'chapel of ease' until the parish of Hebden Bridge was belatedly established in 1844. It would seem they remained also-rans not only in the competition for souls, but also when it came to procuring the best site for a place of worship. A letter of 1824 from a local landowner to the Church Commissioners complains that 'the Methodists, always on the alert on these occasions', had already begun building on the 'the best Site that could be found for the proposed Church'.*

The Established Church simply wasn't in the game. The serious competition for souls and maybe also for building sites lay between the Wesleyans and the Baptists.

Hebden Bridge's new parish church, in its delightful but out-of-town (Mytholm) location. Engraving from an 1840s painting. (PHDA-HLS05080)

The 1851 census had included religious affiliation, something later censuses curiously didn't repeat. It gives a good idea of how the denominations divided up in the Todmorden district, and the omnipresence in the landscape of places of worship. For the Wesleyan Methodists it listed eleven, with 21.8 per cent of total attenders. Smaller Wesleyan offshoots had twelve places of worship, also 21 per cent of attenders. Baptists of the General and Particular persuasion had twelve places of worship and 27.5 per cent. The Church of England struggled with just seven places of worship and 18.1 per cent.[5]

---

* The letter also complains that they have been, to use a modern term, gazumped financially. The Methodists 'have obtained a considerable proportion of the Endowment of the Church'. The suggestion is that the Methodists (Wesleyans) got there first and thereby cornered both the congregation and the financial support that a situation in the centre of town might have garnered. Whether the Wesleyans had any such motive in mind we can't say. But had an Anglican church been built on the Salem site the town would have looked, and felt, very different.

Men and women might be equal before God but 'there was often a social class difference between Wesleyan and Primitive congregations. Where the industrialists were prominent among the Wesleyans, the Primitives had strong working-class support.'[6] Of the 18,000 seats available in all places of worship, '11,000 of the sittings were appropriated, nearly all bought or rented'.

We don't have the figures for Hebden Bridge's Salem Chapel, but the Todmorden chapel had 578 appropriated (whereby you paid in advance for your seat), and just 300 free. God didn't always come cheap. There was no grant-in-aid from parliament for building chapels, as there was for building Anglican churches. But chapel members were the nouveaux riches of their time, and well able to provide the necessary finance. Nor, I'm sure, were they different from any other generation in their concern for status.

Outreach

Belief wasn't of course confined to Sunday services and sermons. 'As the cathedrals of Nonconformity were rising to dispute the dominance of the urban landscape with its mills and mill chimneys, their societies were extending their role into secular affairs. The temperance movement grew in strength and Bands of Hope were formed all over the area …'[7] By 1891 the Band of Hope movement had about 2 million members out of 8 million young people in the country. The Spencer children would have signed the pledge at an early age.

Libraries had an ever-growing role. 'Most of the larger Sunday Schools had lending libraries, originally to serve the small army of Sunday School teachers but developing into a resource for the whole chapel or church community.' In addition, 'nearly every chapel had a mutual improvement society attached', and Salem was no exception. The March 1855 issue of the *Todmorden and Hebden Bridge Historical Almanack* has a reference to the 'Hebden Bridge Wesleyan Mutual Improvement Society'.

Subversion

I've looked in vain for a subversive side to the Spencer family. They kept themselves well buttoned. It took their daughter, Lilian, to break the mould, and that was in 1901. More than forty years before 'Marriage: A lecture' had been the Saturday evening entertainment in the Wesleyan Schoolroom. The date was 4th October 1856. The tone was stern: if in married life a couple don't find happiness 'they must submit to the penalty of their folly'.

The lecture continues in fearsome, admonitory style: 'If, unfortunately, they have ill-advisedly, lightly, or thoughtlessly entered into this relationship, and in their married life they have not found that happiness in each other's society which they once anticipated, they must submit to the penalty of their folly, for they are so related to each other that no disappointed hopes, no want of congeniality, no failing of temper, can have the power to terminate their relationship.'

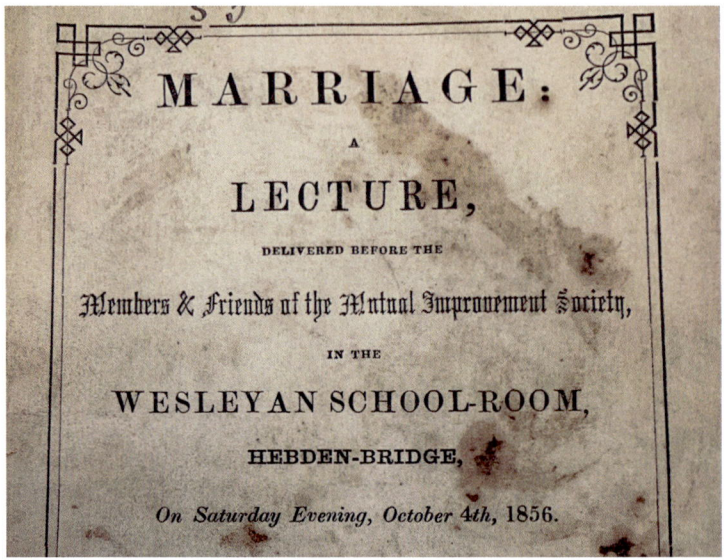

Marriage for one member of the Spencer family, all those years later, was indeed not to be entered into lightly, and indeed, in her case, not at all.

4
Growing Up

Schools and Sunday schools

Chapels were first and foremost places of worship. But they also had Sunday schools attached, and it is impossible to underrate their importance in the days when education outside chapel or church was haphazard at best.

For Joseph's parents, Thomas and Mary, growing up in the 1820s and 1830s, the options would have included 'dame' schools, maybe in a weaving family's kitchen, where learning to read may have been the limit to ambition, or a small private school. But poor schooling would matter less if reading and writing were skills already in the family. Parents would teach, and in turn they would teach their children. As they may have done for Thomas and Mary.

This would probably also apply to Emily's father, Thomas. He is listed in the 1851 census as a 'carder (cotton)', his wife a bonnet maker. A carder would probably be a mill worker. Any education he enjoyed would have been before the 1844 Factory Act reduced the hours that children aged eight to thirteen were allowed to be employed and raised the educational requirement for children to a minimum of three hours a day.

It's helpful to draw in Joseph Greenwood's experience in this context. 'His formal education was limited, he recalled, to nine months' attendance at a "very indifferent children's school". It was his father who taught him to read and write, and who also taught him arithmetic.'[1]

Thomas Walton was, as we've seen, illegitimate: there's no father listed. But his mother's later marriage to a successful local businessman suggests that she could read and write, and she may have taught her son.

For the majority of families, however, where the parents had no education, Sunday schools were only place they could hope to learn the basics. There were forty-nine Sunday schools in the Todmorden area in 1833, with nearly 10,000 enrolments, approximately half in Methodist schools (mostly I'm assuming Wesleyan). But they had one very serious limitation, their focus was on religious knowledge and reading. Writing indeed had initially been 'suppressed by the Wesleyans as a profanation of the Sabbath'.[2] And while attitudes had mellowed since John Wesley's time, strict discipline was the order of the day.

The Wesleyans at the Doghouse chapel (on Doghouse Lane) in Todmorden seemed initially to have been an exception. A report issued in 1818 on their new Sunday school referred to great progress being made in reading and writing. However, minutes from teachers' meetings reveal that reading, spelling and religious instruction were the focus, not writing. An inspector reporting on Todmorden in 1848 stated that while 'three out of four might know how to read, not one in ten could sign their own name'.[3] There's no reason to assume that Hebden Bridge was in any way different.

The prevalence of Nonconformity and the relative isolation of the area meant that Todmorden and Hebden Bridge seem to have been left behind when it came to the government grants (under, for example, the 1833 Factory Act) for schoolhouses and the funding of teachers. But, if nothing more, the principle if not the practice that writing should be taught was by now well established. The world had moved on from the sentiments of the late eighteenth-century Sunday school pioneer, Hannah More, who would allow 'no writing' for the poor. They were not made to be 'scholars and philosophers'. 'It was considered cruelty not kindness to educate a child beyond his station.'[4]

Joseph and Emily

What kind of education would have been available to the next generation, to the children of the Spencer and Walton families, to Joseph and Emily, born in 1854 and 1855? They benefitted from a radical change of sentiment of which Samuel Smiles was the pre-eminent example. Where it had been 'considered cruelty not kindness to educate a child beyond his station', Smiles' book *Self-help*, published in 1859, and a defining Victorian text, reflected a very different mood: 'The poor man's remedy lay in his own hands. If he was only hard-working, thrifty and determined, he could do anything.'[4]

Options had been widening, albeit slowly. 'National' (Church of England) schools were first established in the 1810s along with non-denominational 'British schools'. There were 17,000 National schools in the country by 1851 but it was 1871 before a Church school opened in Hebden Bridge.[5] There is no mention of a British school in the immediate area: the closest seems to have been in Cornholme, on the further side of Todmorden.

More positive for the area had been the 1844 Factory Act which, as we've seen, specified three hours' teaching a day for children aged eight to thirteen. Mill children were known as 'half-timers', spending the morning or afternoon in school. This assumes that the schools were available to teach them, and one effect was indeed to stimulate the growth of private schools, and also factory schools. Two were local, at Lumb Mill near Heptonstall, and Foster Mill in Hebden Bridge, which Emily Walton, as she then was, probably attended.[6]

A Wesleyan day school opened in Hebden Bridge in the 1860s but this would appear to be the school at Walker Lane Chapel on the hillside above the town.[7] But there is also the 'Academy for boys and girls' referred to in Dickenson's history of the Salem chapel. It offered 'sound and careful tuition' and exerted a 'high moral influence'. As late as 1924 when Dickenson wrote his short history many still had 'grateful memories'.[8] Dickenson also mentions 'numerous boarders of both sexes'. Where they might have been lodged is unclear.

Even if the formal establishment of the Academy may have been after Joseph and Emily had passed school age it's clear there was already a well-established commitment to education at Salem Chapel. There's also a record of a day school at the Cross Lanes Wesleyan Chapel, just up the road, in 1857: this would have been the 'Hollinrake's School' which had 140 pupils in 1861, where Henry Hollinrake was one of two teachers.[9]

It could be that it was through their schooling at Salem, both weekday and Sunday, that Joseph and Emily got to know each other.

We have specific evidence for Joseph's close involvement as a young man with the Sunday school at Salem Chapel. The *Todmorden Advertiser and Hebden Bridge Newsletter* of 2nd January 1874 reported that 450 had tea at Salem Wesleyan School, and that 'secretary Joseph Spencer read the report'. He would have been no more than nineteen years old.

It was later that year, in November, that the new Sunday school building opened. The previous year, in August, the laying of the cornerstone had been celebrated in style. A procession, flags and banners, with the local brass band leading the way, marked this as many another big occasion.*

'Shortly after noon there was a large gathering of friends and scholars; the procession being formed, the children carrying flags and banners, it marched through the village headed by the Hebden Bridge Brass Band.' (Note the reference to 'village' rather than 'town', even though town status had been granted in 1866.) On the hillsides people who could not hear what was said 'could at least ... hear the singing'.

---

* The history of Salem chapel refers to two other reasons, other than the numbers attending, for building a new Sunday school. 'The system of placing Sunday Schools under Chapels was once very common, but it was not conducive to the health of the scholars, nor are they as attractive as Schools ought to be.'

Queen Victoria's Diamond Jubilee procession, 1897, with the local Wesleyan Sunday School in the lead. This photo is from up the hill in Heptonstall. (PHDA-HLS05146)

The outreach of the Wesleyans and Baptists, and the Established Church, could only extend so far. Private and factory schools as we've seen catered for half-timers. But the importance of improving standards was recognised at a national level by the 1870 Education Act. The years, indeed decades, that followed saw radical change. (See pages 114–115) The first non-denominational 'board school', financed out of an education rate, opened in Hebden Bridge in 1877, in temporary premises – the Salem Sunday School schoolroom. The year 1878 saw the opening of the purpose-built school at Stubbings. It was not before time: an inspector's report of 1876 'commented that only half of the half-timers in Hebden Bridge had reached the fourth standard by the age of thirteen, "owing to the imperfect methods" of the private schools which many of them attended'.[10]

By this time Joseph and Emily would have been courting. They must have discussed, given all this ferment, what options there would be for their own children.

Marriage

Joseph married Emily at Salem Wesleyan Chapel, Hebden Bridge, on 30th August 1877. The marriage is recorded in the Spencer family Bible, which dates from this time. The chapel demolished in 1975 was the chapel built in 1885, so Joseph and Emily's marriage would have taken place in an earlier chapel (built 1824, see photo on page 17) on the site. The adjacent Salem Mill, later known as Melbourne Mill, was demolished in 1983. The Co-op now stands on the site.

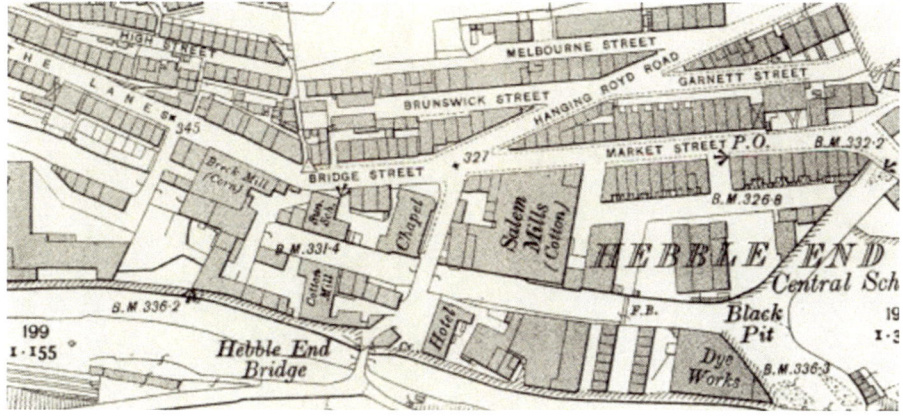

Ordnance Survey map of 1905. The Lanes (also known as Bridge Lanes), Bridge Street and Market Street mark the road running west to east through the town. High Street is top left and Salem Wesleyan Chapel is in the centre, to the left of Salem Mills. Reproduced with the permission of the National Library of Scotland. [11]

A Family Tree of the Spencer and Walton Families

also showing the relationship between Edward and James Kershaw and the Spencer family

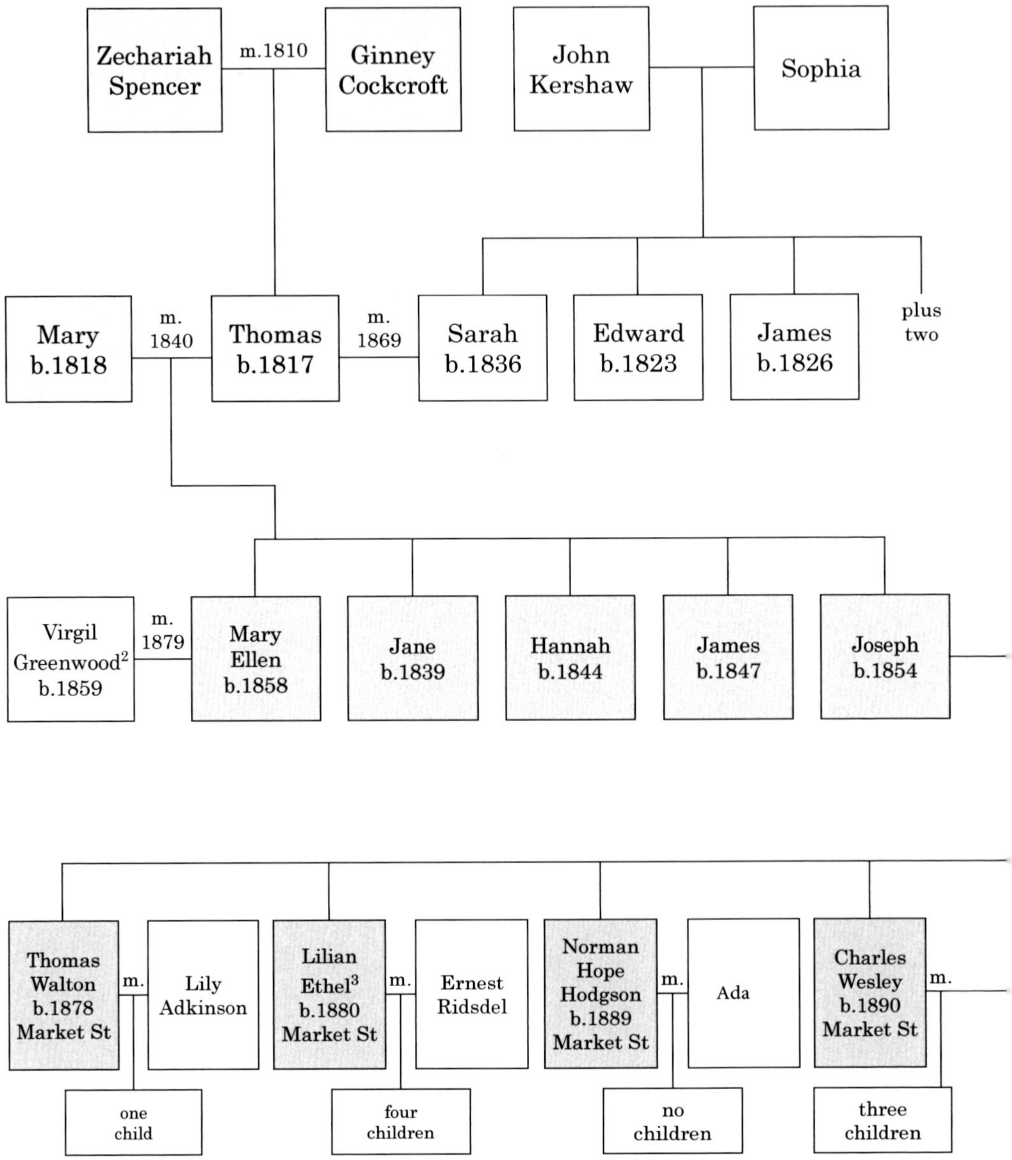

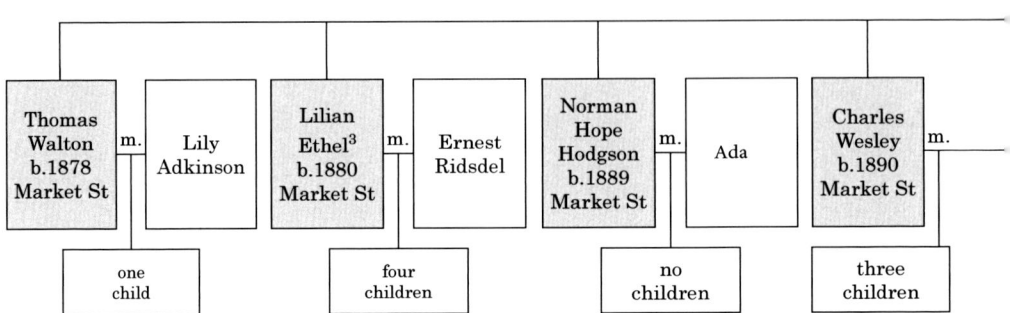

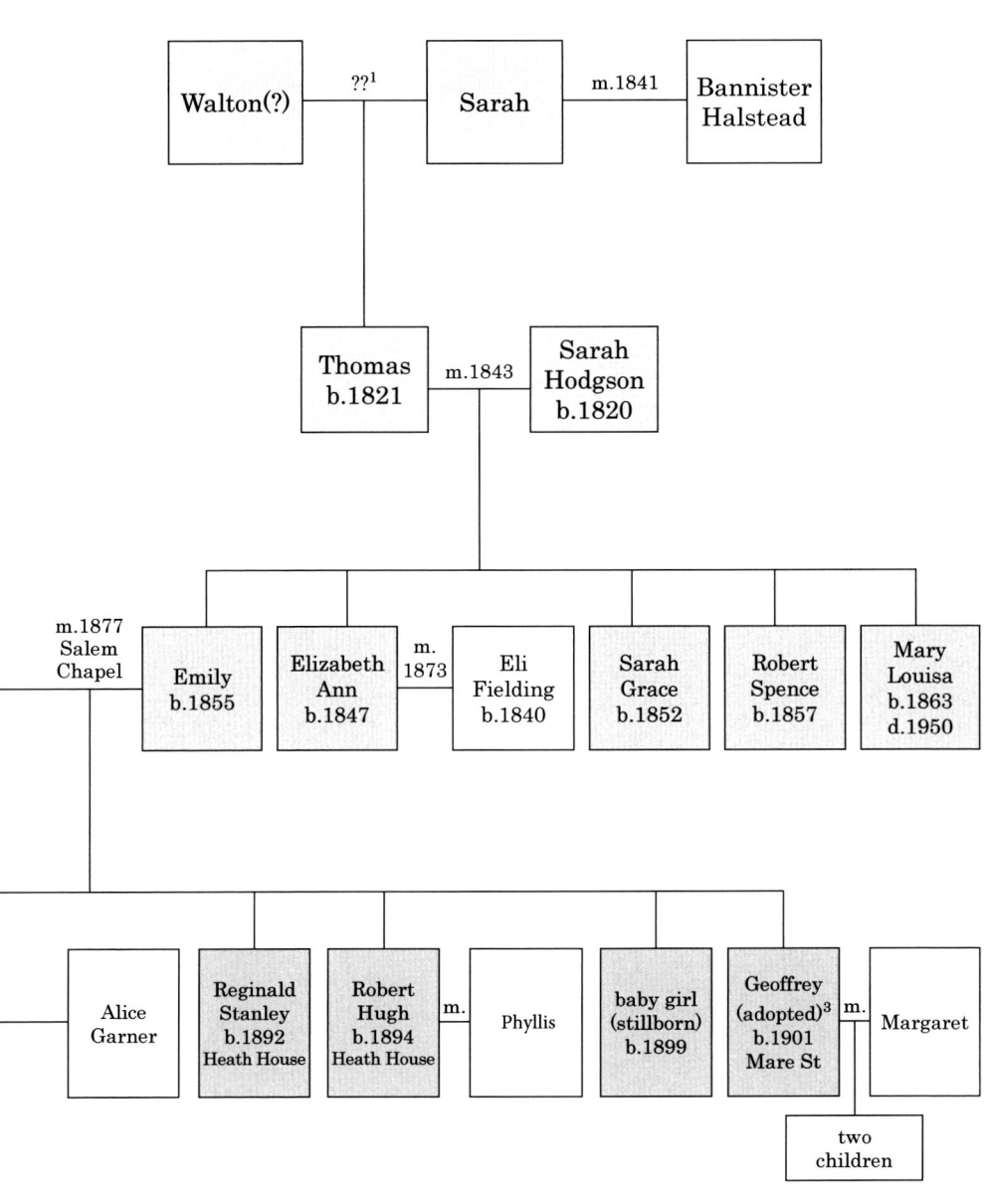

[1] No father listed in the register when Thomas married Sarah Hodgson in 1843
[2] Eldest son of Joseph Greenwood, manager, Nutclough Mill
[3] Lilian gave birth to Geoffrey in 1901, in Mare Street, London. Father unknown. Adopted by his grandparents, Joseph and Emily

5

The Waltons of Foster Mill

It helps who you marry. And Joseph Spencer married well. He, as we've seen, made a good impression in chapel circles at a young age. Many of the more senior chapel members were local businessmen and they were among Joseph's early supporters. The Protestant or, better, the Nonconformist work ethic, was very much in evidence. Joseph was a bright lad, no doubt prepared to put in the work. And one consequence was a good marriage, to Emily, the daughter of one of the bosses at Foster Mill, by name Thomas Walton.

Another marriage connection must have helped. Joseph was connected to the Kershaw family by way of his father's second marriage to Sarah Kershaw. Sarah's brother James and Thomas Walton were business associates. (See page 78.) More on the Kershaws later.

Thomas Walton

The occupations of Emily's father, Thomas Walton, and mother, Sarah, are recorded in the 1851 census as carder and bonnet maker respectively. A carder prepared yarn for spinning by brushing with wire pads so that all the fibres ran in the same direction. Bonnet making may well have been an outsourced activity. She could have been working from home, or in a tailor's shop.

Thomas, as a carder, would have been aware of the success of another Walton, James Walton, born in 1803 in nearby Ripponden, who 'in the early 1830s … developed a new form of wire-card for use in textile manufacturing'. In 1853 'he established the company of James Walton & Sons, supplying machinery and cards to the textile industry of Great Britain and beyond. The factory was the largest of its kind in the world.'[1]

Thomas Walton's work as carder was on a somewhat smaller scale. But he also had ambition. In 1854, and probably before then, he was working at Foster Mill (of which more later) and in the 1861 census he's described as manager of a cotton mill, which would have been Foster Mill. In 1871 he is 'manager and manufacturer', with an address of 1 Foster Lane.

We can assume he had a big influence on his son-in-law. He died aged fifty-six and his wife Sarah, daughters Sarah and Mary Louisa, and son Robert Spence Walton followed him, over the years, to the same grave. (See Appendix One.)

Hebden Bridge looking north from across the Calder, c.1880, with Foster Mill prominent above the town. (PHDA-ALC00405)

Throughout his life he was closely involved with Salem Chapel, where he was a steward as far back as 1844. He continued in that role until immediately before his death in 1877. He was also a local preacher of some standing. The *Todmorden Advertiser and Hebden Bridge Newsletter* has the following from 1st August 1868:

> 'SCHOOL SERMONS – On Sunday, the anniversary sermons of the Wesleyan School, Lane-bottom, were preached by Mr Thos. Walton, of Foster-mill, Hebden-bridge, afternoon and evening. The collection amounted to £12 4s 6d.'

The (Wesleyan) Local Preachers Benevolent Aid Association was it seems a very active body, operating on a national level. The local branch had a travelling expenses fund for which Thomas Walton was the 'dispenser'. He was, one can surmise, someone who liked to be in control.[2]

A much earlier Thomas Walton reference appears in a 4th June 1853 report in the *Halifax Courier* of the first annual meeting of the Hebden Bridge Gas Company. He is proposing a vote of thanks to the directors. This would make sense if he was, as is possible, already employed at Foster Mill.

There had been complaints about slow progress at the meeting but, the report continues, 'when the cottages had ceased to burn farthing candles, when shopkeepers displayed their beautiful goods, by the aid of brilliant gas, when the tradesmen and middle class displaced the tallow by gas, and when the mansions of the aristocracy became as illuminated as the sun, then the shareholders might look upon their scrip certificates as tinged with the gold of California, or as the importation of the diggings from Australia.'

(The diggings of Australia retain their value, 170 years later. Not so the gold of California.)

It was on a related subject that Thomas wrote, in September 1871, to the Hebden Bridge Local Board, 'asking them to allow the lamp at Foster-mill to be lighted as formerly: stating that it had been discontinued lighting out of spite and malice, which had now passed away from the Board'. The wording is a little muddled but the outcome was good: the lamp was relit, as a public lamp.[3]

What is unusual about this report is the display of temper it mentions. Thomas Walton was not someone to be trifled with. Whether his daughter, Emily, was of a similar disposition we can't say.

The only other evidence of his activities at Foster Mill I've located in the local press are notices of job vacancies from December 1872, inviting responses to 'Mr Walton of Foster Mill'.

Dr Spence Walton

Thomas's son, and Emily's brother, Dr Robert Spence Walton (always known as Spence), received the diploma of MB (Bachelor of Medicine) from London University in 1880, initially practising in Scarborough before returning to Hebden Bridge.

We've no record of where he lived in London. He was enrolled on a three-year course. For a young man from a relatively poor home to take a degree in London would have been a radical step.

As well as everyday medical concerns he would have been aware of the danger from epidemics, not least typhoid, typhus and smallpox. The Public Health Act of 1875 encompassed water supply and sewage and contagious diseases. Spence would have been up to the mark. The terrible typhus (carried by fleas) epidemic in Heptonstall Slack (see above) was a recent memory. Typhoid being waterborne would also be an ever-present concern. Sanitation was a big issue in Hebden Bridge (see page 65), and it didn't get its own sewage works until 1900.

There are multiple references to him in the press over the period 1888 to 1908, many referring to accidents to which he was called, with the occasional graphic description of, for example, a bad fall by one of the workers constructing Walshaw Dean reservoir.[4]

'The first of February 1896, will long be remembered by the residents of Hebden Bridge, the occasion being the reception and formal presentation of an ambulance carriage to the town ... The carriage is fitted-up with the most modern appliances, and capable of carrying two persons at a time.' The event was marked by 'a procession of the local lodges of Odd-fellows and Foresters, fire brigade, ambulance carriage and ambulance men, and Hebden Bridge and Heptonstall brass bands'. We can assume it would have been called upon often by Dr Walton, and it would no doubt after a little while have lost its remarkably pristine appearance.[5]
(PHDA-ALC08288)

The family connection, with a brother who was a doctor, would have been a reassurance for Emily and Joseph, bringing up a young family. Spence lived with his sister, Mary, who also never married, and his mother, Sarah, at Salem Buildings, Market Street, adjacent to the chapel, until retiring to Fylde on the Lancashire coast. A 'sale of work' at Salem Chapel in December 1901 refers to 'Doctor and Miss Walton [receiving] the guests'.[6]

He was also a member of the Hebden Bridge Liberal Club: he's mentioned in a report from February 1902 along with John Crowther, Eli Fielding and Joseph Greenwood, all of whom were as we will see significant figures in Joseph Spencer's life. The meeting touched on the Boer War and 'condemned the government', and then focused on a new Licensing Law

Dr Robert Spence Walton, known as Spence, from the Spencer family album (see page 142). He appears to be about to go on his rounds, with his coat and in his right hand a top hat which it seems was de rigueur for doctors at the time.

Reform Bill. The secretary was 'glad to say that clubs like this against which there was no taint whatsoever of scandal would not be affected by the bill'.[7]

Dr Walton was also a mason, and Worshipful Master of the Prince George Masonic Lodge in 1907.[8] 'The installing master was George Pickles of Hebden Bridge and a large number of Hebden Bridge brethren were present.' It may also be that he followed in his father's footsteps as a local preacher. He died in 1920.

The big fire

One of the most impressive mills in the Hebden Valley, 'seventeen windows long, six wide, and six storeys high', must have been Foster Mill. It operated as an old-style cotton mill, with as many as 20,000 spindles. Thomas Walton had been dead over ten years when in 1888 a major fire reduced the mill to a shell. The emotional impact on the family would have been considerable. Thomas Spencer would have been ten years old, his sister, Lilian, eight.

Foster Mill after the fire in 1888. Compare the photo on page 29 to appreciate the impact the blaze would have had on the town. (PHDA-RDA00152)

Horses brought a steam fire engine down from Todmorden, but it was too little and too late. Before 9 o'clock the flames had burnt through the roof, 'making a glare which could be distinctly seen four or five miles away ... by 9.10 the roof began to fall and as it tumbled in large sections it caused a noise almost like thunder, followed by a terrific outburst of flames into the sky.'[9]

The Mytholmroyd fire brigade, 1901, an earlier incarnation of which we can assume was called to the Foster Mill fire. The narrow alleyway adds drama to proceedings. (Jack Uttley Photo Library)

It had at least been 'insured in various offices, and it is expected that a great part if not all the loss will be covered'. It was the third big fire on the site, with earlier fires in 1828 and 1853. The immediate impact may have been lessened by the fact that it was, as a cotton mill, no longer a popular place to work. 'The 150 hands were generally strangers, the natives of the town mostly preferring the employment offered by the ready-made clothing establishments.'

Ready-made became its focus after the fire when it was bought in 1890 and rebuilt by the Redman Brothers. They were already by that year employing 600–700 people across the town and manufacturing 15,000 garments per week.[10] They had started their business in 1879. In a different incarnation, it was at Foster Mill that the fustian weavers' strike that lasted from 1906 to 1908 began, of which more later. The mill was finally demolished in 1985.

6

Connections

At the time of the 1871 census the family is still living at the High Street address. Joseph, aged sixteen, is already described as a tailor, working as an apprentice. His father, Thomas, is still listed as a fustian cutter.

The coming of the railway had been the great catalyst. As a shoemaker in 1841 Thomas may have found the railway brought in product from outside, restricting opportunity. Fustian on the other hand progressively opened up new markets – and new opportunities. Thomas and his new wife, Sarah, his first wife having died, would have had ambitions for Joseph. Thomas had married Sarah in 1869, when Joseph would have been fourteen.

Sarah, then aged forty-four and a spinster, was a member of the Kershaw family, with two older brothers, Edward and James, sons of John Kershaw, all of them successful tailors. The Kershaws were one of several firms run by family and friends, all with Salem Chapel connections, who gave Joseph their backing. Others included the firms of John Crowther and Eli Fielding, of whom more below.

John Kershaw and Sons

The 1851 census listed John Kershaw as a woollen draper. His two sons were both in the family business. James took over the firm from his father, while Edward moved over the border to Lancashire and built a successful business there, with branches 'at Rochdale, Oldham, Shaw and Ashton, and elsewhere'. The connection between James Kershaw and Joseph Spencer was to be the most important of Joseph's working life. In a very different way the connection with Edward was also to be important, even beyond the grave, something we will return to later. In 1874 Edward moved south, to Effingham in Surrey, and James took over his brother's business.[1]

As a strong Wesleyan, James was very much involved in the affairs of Salem Chapel and indeed the wider community: he was a member of the Hebden Bridge Local Board from 1871. He was a good person to have on your side.

We touched on William Barker's business in an earlier chapter. James had his own claim, along with his father, to have been the first wholesale clothier in the town. In 1866 the firm had advertised for 'machine hands' and eighteen months later they began selling sewing machines. (See earlier, page 12.)

Some twenty years later, in 1886, while proposing a toast to the town at the White Horse Hotel James claimed 'that his firm [as John Kershaw and Sons] was the first to introduce sewing machines into this neighbourhood'. A report from the same period in the *Hebden Bridge Times* records his claim that 'he could trace the whole of the tailoring establishments in Hebden Bridge as having risen from the establishment to which he belonged'.

*

At what point Joseph joined John Kershaw and Sons as an apprentice isn't clear. There couldn't have been a better introduction to the clothing trade. Advertisements throughout the 1870s describe the firm as 'wholesale and woollen drapers, tailors, hatters and general outfitters'. What is striking is the reach of the business. 'Rochdale, Oldham, Shaw, and Ashton, and elsewhere' are mentioned in one context, Hebden Bridge, Burnley and Manchester in another. Joseph would have been encouraged from an early stage to look beyond Hebden Bridge, and to look west, into Lancashire, rather than east to the Ridings.

> **JOHN KERSHAW AND SONS,**
> The Lanes, Hebden-bridge, 10, Brown-street, Burnley, and 23, Bradford-road, Manchester,
> Wholesale & Retail Woollen Drapers, Tailors, Hatters & General Outfitters,
> WOOLLEN MERCHANTS AND WAREHOUSEMEN.
> A Choice Selection of CLOTHS FOR OVERCOATS in various Makes and Colours.
> FANCY CLOTHS IN GREAT VARIETY, Suitable for all Occasions.
> Also, a LARGE STOCK OF BLACK, Broads and Narrows, West of England and Yorkshire Makes.
> **AGENTS FOR ALL KINDS OF SEWING MACHINES.**

The emphasis in this advertisement for John Kershaw and Sons from September 1877 is on 'cloths for overcoats'.[2] And they are 'woollen merchants'. No cotton-based fabrics. No mention of fustian. It doesn't specify what kind of 'fancy cloths' they had on offer.

Joseph was to build his business in the 1880s around the growing demand for smarter, more fashionable clothes. John Kershaw's focus seems to have been less on tailoring, more on the supply of cloth, including 'blacks, broads and narrows', and indeed of sewing machines as well.

Throughout the decade the two businesses operated in parallel, usually advertising together. The last advertisement I have traced for John Kershaw and Sons dates to 1889 and carried the strapline 'cheap and fashionable tailoring' – maybe not a description Joseph would have chosen.

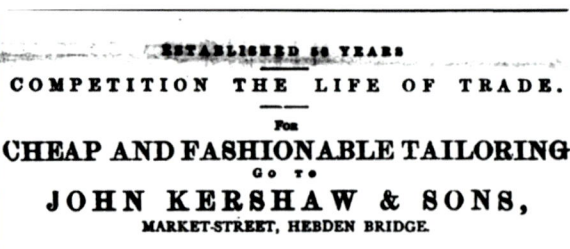

John Crowther

James Kershaw, as we've seen, argued that his business had been the true trailblazer for the ready-made industry in Hebden Bridge. Joseph Crowther and John, his younger brother by a few years, might have disputed that claim.

At some point in the early 1860s Joseph 'had decided to go it alone and he created a sewing workshop in Hangingroyd Lane'. He died young, age thirty-five, in 1875. The business was put up for auction at the White Horse Hotel. What is striking is the large attendance, 'including tradesmen from Halifax, Bradford, Leeds, Manchester and Bolton'. It's an indication of the reach of his business.

The auction notwithstanding, his younger brother, John, took over and by 1881 the business as a wholesale clothier is recorded as having 150 workers. John built himself a new house in Mytholm, Heath House, and it was there that Joseph Spencer moved with his family in 1890. John Crowther, like James Kershaw, was closely associated with Salem Chapel. He was, in 1896, elected vice-chairman of the newly constituted Hebden Bridge School Board. The photos of John and his wife, Mary, are taken from the Spencer family album, as are the photos of Eli Fielding and his wife, Elizabeth Ann, below.

John Crowther.

Mary Crowther.

The Spencer family album, with photographs inserted in decorated pages, has just twenty-six photos. We don't have an exact date but all the photographs are of family and friends with a Hebden Bridge connection. They appear to have been taken about the time of the Spencers' departure from Hebden Bridge in 1901 or 1902, though the inclusion of Beatrice Fielding as a young woman suggests a date closer to 1910. It may be that the photographs were collected into an album about that time. Where photographs are of people who can be identified they appear in the main text. Where their subjects are unidentified they're reproduced in Appendix Two.

Eli Fielding

Eli Fielding appears in the same album. He had a successful business as a cotton spinner, employing, according to the 1881 census, ninety-six people. In 1901 the family address is listed as West End. The 1911 census records Eli and Elizabeth as living in Blackpool. He was Joseph's brother-in-law, fifteen years older than Joseph, and married to Emily's older sister, Elizabeth Ann. Where John Crowther helped out with housing, Eli helped Joseph out financially. He is mentioned in the context of the first mortgage Joseph Spencer took out in 1884: the suggestion is that he was the primary source of funds. His name also recurs in later mortgages taken out by Joseph.

Eli and Elizabeth Ann Fielding.

Beatrice, their daughter.

7
Setting Up Shop

The Spencers' first child, Thomas[1], was born in 1878 at Salem House, presumably one of the houses adjacent to the old Wesleyan chapel. Their daughter, Lilian, followed, born in 1880 at a 'Market Street' address, probably also Salem House. A minute of the Waterworks Committee, charging Joseph Spencer 1/-, would seem to confirm that this was their address at the time.[2] Emily's mother, Sarah Walton (Thomas having died in 1877), may have been living with them.

Joseph and Emily, with their children, Thomas and Lilian, c.1882.

In the 1881 census Joseph is listed as an 'outfitter tailor' in Market Street, next door to Handel Halstead. Handel Halstead's houses (three houses are listed in an 1872 plan in Calderdale Archives) were opposite the Wesleyan chapel, adjacent to Barker's Terrace.[3] There is another family connection here, Emily's grandmother having married Bannister Halstead in 1843.

Looking down Bridge Lanes toward Salem Wesleyan Chapel bottom right, c.1910, a few years after the family left the town. This would have been the route Joseph took to work from Heath House, and the family took to chapel and school. (PHDA-ALC06352)

It's reasonable to assume that it was in 1881 that Joseph set up on his own. The family would probably have lived above the shop. He would have been twenty-six. The first advertisement for the business appeared in the *Todmorden & District News* the following year, on 24th March 1882. Note the parenthesis '(late of the firm of J. Kershaw & Sons)'.

> **JOSEPH SPENCER,**
> (late of the firm of J. Kershaw & Sons,)
> **MERCHANT TAILOR, HATTER & GENERAL OUTFITTER,**
> **BRIDGE-STREET, HEBDEN-BRIDGE,**
> Begs to call the attention of the public generally, to his entirely NEW and well-assorted STOCK of
> **SPRING AND SUMMER GOODS**
> From West of England and Scotch Manufacturers.
> ———
> GENTS' SUPERIOR SILK AND FELT HATS of the Newest Fashions and from the most Noted Makers.
> LADIES' JACKETS made in all the leading styles.
> ———
> **SPECIAL ATTENTION GIVEN TO MOURNING ORDERS.**

The *Todmorden Advertiser and Hebden Bridge Newsletter* refers to a 30th June meeting that year of the Todmorden (Poor Law) Guardians when 'a letter was read from the clerk to the York Union asking whether there was any objection to binding a pauper boy as apprentice to Mr Joseph Spencer, tailor, of Hebden Bridge'. There was none.

There's also an intriguing small ad from the *Manchester Evening News* of 10th October, asking for 'a first-class machinist'.

> WANTED, a first-class MACHINIST for the tailoring business. Apply Joseph Spencer, outfitter, Hebden Bridge.

'Fashionable shades'

It's clear from his advertisements that Joseph Spencer had ambitions well beyond everyday wear. As well as 'Spring and Summer Goods from the West Country and Scotch Manufacturers' he was advertising 'ladies' jackets made in all the leading styles'. It may be that he was looking for a machinist with skills he couldn't find locally. Joseph on his regular journeys to Manchester would be buying from the extraordinary range of materials available, and making up on his premises, but he would also have been buying finished items, and making alterations as required.

Setting up on your own would not have been expensive. 'A small amount of capital equipment was needed to commence production; a sewing machine (costing between £4 and £14 in 1880) was the most expensive item.'[4] But employing staff would have taken the business to another level.

Joseph was still renting, as workplace and home, at a Market Street address in 1884, according to the electoral register. His advertisements always appeared beneath those for John Kershaw and Sons. They are in effect a joint placement, and suggests their businesses were complementary. Where Joseph Spencer announces himself as a 'Tailor' and 'embraces the most fashionable materials', John Kershaw and Sons is content to describe its business as 'Outfitters', with no additional copy.

The materials Joseph highlighted in an advertisement in December 1884 (below) were 'fashionable shades of meltons, beavers, naps, worsteds, etc'.[5] He was already clear, by the age of twenty-nine, what his direction of travel as a business would be. And, to put it in geographical terms, that was west and south-west.*

> **JOSEPH SPENCER,**
> **MERCHANT TAILOR, HEBDEN-BRIDGE,**
> is now showing an entirely
> **NEW STOCK OF AUTUMN AND WINTER GOODS,**
> embracing the most
> **FASHIONABLE SHADES OF MELTONS, BEAVERS, NAPs, WORSTEDS, &c.,**
> Also the
> **NEW SHADES IN WORSTEDS AND MELTONS FOR LADIES' JACKETS AND ULSTERS.**
>
> **MOURNING ORDERS PROMPTLY EXECUTED.**

---

* Joseph's customers could differentiate between the different kinds of cloth he offered. Not all of us today have this level of expertise. For information on the different materials see Appendix Four.

Another advertisement in the same paper from a few months later (27th March 1885) refers to 'branch offices', the first time that they're mentioned.

> BRANCH OFFICES:—
> 95, BRADFORD-ROAD, MANCHESTER, & 6, ROBERT-STREET, BURNLEY.

Joseph, as his mentor James, and James's brother, Edward, before him, was heading over the border. It seems he never thought of looking east, to Halifax, only west, to Lancashire, and to the heart of the cotton trade, to Manchester.

8

Taking The Train

John Kershaw, as noted above, had branches in Hebden Bridge, Burnley, Manchester and Otley. Joseph followed in his mentor's footsteps. For both businesses the railway was the great facilitator, opening up communication between the Calder Valley and Manchester and the Lancashire cotton towns in a remarkable way. The Manchester and Leeds Railway, which ran through Todmorden, Hebden Bridge and Sowerby Bridge, had fully opened in 1841. In 1847 it became the Lancashire and Yorkshire Railway (LYR), later merging with other lines to become the London, Midland and Scottish Railway.

Branch lines followed almost immediately. There was a rail connection between Burnley and Accrington as early as 1844 (originally the 'Blackburn, Burnley, Accrington and Colne Extension Railway'). In 1849 a single-line branch opened (doubled in 1860) from Todmorden to Burnley. A branch line taking the railway into the centre of Oldham opened in 1847. It's curious to note how the early railway carriages could mimic the old stagecoaches in their appearance.

The Rochdale Canal, the sections of which from Sowerby Bridge to Rochdale had opened in 1798, had been a wonder for its time but operated of course at a much slower pace. Prior to that, all commercial traffic across the Pennines (to Rochdale and Burnley) had followed the turnpike route operated by a trust authorised under a Turnpike Act of 1760. All other distance travel was by packhorse routes until in the early 1800s further turnpike routes, including the Cragg Vale Turnpike in 1815, were authorised.

A rail journey of twenty-eight miles to Manchester Victoria Station taking about an hour would have seemed revolutionary. From Market Street, Hebden Bridge it wasn't more than a few minutes' walk to Hebden Bridge Station. Likewise, from Manchester Victoria to Market Street, Manchester.

The railway not only reduced travelling time, but also standardised it. Another recent invention, the telegraph, allowed the different railway companies to adjust their time and their timetables to Greenwich Mean Time.[1] The Liverpool and Manchester Railway was one of the first out of the gate, ordering the adjustment of clocks to GMT at both its Liverpool and Manchester stations in January 1846. The LYR, operating out of the same station, would have followed shortly afterwards.[2]

The Kershaws had taken full advantage of these railway connections in

TAKING THE TRAIN

Two prints based on paintings by A. F. Tait, showing the route taken by the railway, both c.1845, one looking down-valley, with Hebden Bridge station middle distance, the other looking up-valley beyond Hebden Bridge parish church, toward Todmorden, with mill chimneys barely visible. (PHDA-HLS00169 and HLH06102)

building their businesses and Joseph was to do the same. Burnley, Accrington and Oldham were all towns where he opened shops.

Joseph's premises in the early stages were at Manchester and Burnley. The Bradford Road address (close to where the Etihad Stadium is today) was two miles from Manchester Victoria Station where the Hebden Bridge train departed. The rapidly extending tram service meant the city centre was only minutes away. It may have doubled as a storeroom and shop.

Manchester, Mosley Street, before 1896. (Reproduced from Mercantile Manchester)

It would have been his stepping-off point for venturing into the big city. Just how important the tram network was for Manchester cannot be underestimated. By 1882 the network operated by the Manchester Carriage Company and covering the wider Manchester area extended to more than seventy-five miles, growing to 140 miles by 1900. Bradford Road, where Joseph had his first office, was one of nineteen depots. The service involved 515 trams and over 5,000 horses. Either side of 1900 saw a major transformation as electricity replaced horsepower.[3]

A Manchester electric tram, c.1900. (Francis Frith Collection)

9

Putting Down Roots

New premises

Joseph it seems was looking to put down a marker, and plans to develop further east along Market Street gave him the opportunity. A conveyance of 17th June 1884 (Joseph would have been thirty) records the sale of land on Market Street, whereby he pays £287 to William Kitchen and £450 to Mortimer and James Moss (Moss Brothers) for 'all those three several plots *or* parcels of land or ground part of a close of land called Salem Holme formerly Black Pit Holme in Hebden Bridge ... being or comprising Lots 23, 24 and 25 at a sale by Public Auction at the White Horse Hotel in Hebden Bridge aforesaid on the 23rd September 1880 ...'[1]

Associated with this is an indenture dated two days later, relating to a mortgage of £500 taken out by Joseph on the Salem Holme plot of land. This is between 'Joseph Spencer, tailor and draper, Eli Fielding of Hebden Bridge, cotton spinner, and William Henry Sutcliffe, Gent'.

Despite the proximity of Halifax there is no mention of a building society as the source of the loan, or later loans. It looks to be Eli Fielding who was lending the money to Joseph. William Henry Sutcliffe (note his status as a 'gentleman') was Joseph's solicitor but he would have been dealing with a clerk rather than Sutcliffe himself.[2]

The same three are referred to in later documents, from 1889, 1895, 1899 and 1902. Eli Fielding, as we've already seen, was Joseph's brother-in-law, married to Emily's much older sister, Elizabeth Ann.

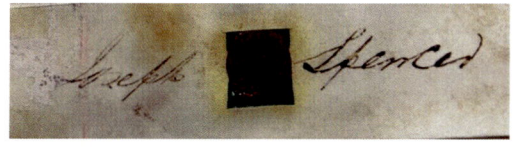

On the back of the 1884 indenture is another, dated 2nd January 1889, referring to a further sum of £350, additional to another £650 recently advanced. Joseph had paid back £300 of the original loan so his total indebtedness at this point was £1,200. At today's values this represents a sum of £98,000 using the National Archives currency calculator, and £158,000 using the Bank of England's inflation calculator. The former may be a more realistic comparison.

A further indenture of 1885, between Joseph, William Henry Sutcliffe and 'John Greenwood of Slack, grocer', records the purchase from Joseph, for the sum of £200, by John Greenwood, of plot 25 of the land purchased by Joseph the previous year.

There is also, in the Calderdale Archives, a plan from December 1887 in the names of 'J. Spencer' and 'J. Greenwood' relating to 'three houses and shops in Market Street'. I'm assuming the preparations for building were already well advanced by this stage.³

'Treat to Workpeople'

It was March 1889, almost five years after his purchase of the land, before 'J. Spencer, Merchant Tailor' could finally move into his new premises at 25 Market Street. It was an occasion for celebration.

The *Todmorden & District News* of 8th March 1889 reported on a 'Treat to Workpeople' given 'to his workpeople and their friends, to the number of about 50, on Tuesday evening last, in his commodious new premises'. The report refers to a 'first-class knife and fork tea … provided by Mr Crabtree, of the Commercial Hotel … Music was provided for dancing, and with games, songs etc, the evening was spent in the most enjoyable manner.'

His double-fronted premises are still there, occupied by Element, a jewellery store.

The party may also have doubled as the annual treat. Annual treats or outings were a feature of many firms. The entertainment would, we can assume, have retained a degree of decorum, the Commercial Hotel being a temperance hotel run by Edward Crabtree at 10 Market Street.

What did the phrase 'commodious new premises' entail? There are big windows in the roof space, no doubt to facilitate the sewing, and these extend to the west, above Element and its immediate neighbour. The two shops (Joseph's being double-fronted) are designed as one building, occupying the land originally bought by Joseph in 1884. Quoins, brickwork, hood moulds and keystones within the second-floor window arches give the building a distinctive character, and there's a fine doorway on the eastern, Hilton Street, side, with a delicate hood mould enclosing an intricately carved date stone.

Immediately above the shop lay living accommodation, with a cutting-out room on the second floor, and separate girls' and men's workrooms on the top floor.

25 Market Street front elevation, from the original plan (later amended) of 1887.

The 'From Fulling to Fustianopolis' website describes the premises as they were in 1917 (by this time occupied by Greenwood Bros):

'24–25 Market Street ... had a second floor cutting room, where patterns were chalked on piled up layers of cloth to be cut out by men using power driven band knives, whilst on the top floor women joined up pieces of garments using sewing machines, and hand-sewing difficult parts.'[4]

The layout of the building may not have changed much over the years, though the cutting out, back in 1889, would not have been done by power-driven band knives.

Market Street, Hebden Bridge, 1890s, looking east. (PHDA-ALC00336)

'Our large stock … embraces the newest things'

Joseph Spencer placed an advertisement in the *Burnley Express* on 23rd July 1887 for his new shop in the town, at No. 1 Yorkshire Street. He'd moved his business from premises in Robert Street. The address suggests a prominent location, and he refers to his already 'numerous customers'.

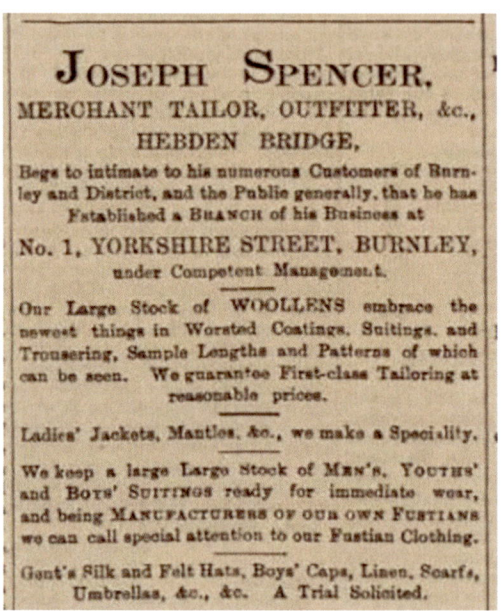

There's a focus on worsted, I assume for leisurewear and smarter occasions. Samples and 'first-class tailoring' are available. Likewise 'silk and felt hats'. Disposable incomes may have been limited, but Joseph Spencer was clearly adept at matching the clothes he sold to a rapidly changing market.

Many of his customers may have been discovering 'fashion' for the first time. He was building his business on a rising if uneven tide of prosperity among the mill workers and the rising middle class of the Pennine towns.

Women's clothing ('Ladies' Jackets, Mantles, &c.') of the time needed more close fitting and would have required his individual attention. But all the while he never lost sight of the importance of fustian, of corduroy and moleskin, for working men, and with his own manufacturing capacity this may still have been a major part of his turnover.

10

Know Your Greenwoods

Greenwood was a popular name in Hebden Bridge.[1] Joseph's neighbour on Market Street, to whom he'd sold the adjacent plot in 1885, was John Greenwood of Slack, described as a grocer. It was another Greenwood, Young Greenwood, a farmer, who bought number 25 from Joseph when he sold the premises at auction in 1907. (See page 134) The company owning the shop in 1917 is listed in *Kelly's Directory* as 'Greenwood Bros', described as a wholesale clothier.

An earlier Greenwood business was James Greenwood's Wholesale Clothiers Limited, whose origins Tom Greenwood recounts in his history of the Hebden Bridge clothing industry.[2]

James Greenwood was setting up his business about the same time as Joseph Spencer. Tom Greenwood describes the launch of the Greenwood business 'as seemingly quite typical of the beginnings of many of the manufacturers'. James began to make garments about 1875 when he was in his early twenties and sold his fustians both retail (branches in Scotland) and wholesale. Previously he had worked, like so many, including Joseph Spencer's parents, as a fustian cutter. He was based at this time in St George's Square.

Joseph Spencer was also making garments, but not for wholesale. Having learnt the retail trade, that remained his focus.

Joseph Greenwood of Nutclough Mill

The best known of the Greenwoods was Joseph Greenwood, founder member of and manager for many years of Hebden Bridge Fustian Co-operative Manufacturing Society, based at Nutclough Mill. Over almost fifty years of independent existence it gained for itself a legendary status.[3]

There was a family connection with the Spencers. Joseph Spencer's younger sister, Mary Ellen, married Virgil Greenwood, the eldest son of Joseph Greenwood. But, while there may have been a family, and maybe a friendly relationship, between the two Josephs, there's no evidence of any working relationship. The Fustian Co-operative was, as Joseph Greenwood stated, producing 'exclusively for co-operative societies'.[4]

A dinner at the White Lion Hotel to celebrate an Annual Stocktaking of the Fustian Co-operative, probably early 1890s. Joseph Greenwood is front row centre. (PHDA-CWS00102)

Virgil Greenwood

In January 1878 Virgil had a bad, and widely reported, accident. 'On Tuesday last, Mr Virgil Greenwood, son of Mr Joseph Greenwood, manager of the Fustian Company, met with what might have proved a very serious matter. He was employed at the Fustian Company's works, Nutclough, and in passing from one side of his frame to the other, the point of the knife came into contact with his body, and the haft end being on the rest, the point pierced his body to the extent of two or three inches. Dr Thomas was called in, and under his treatment Greenwood is recovering.'[5]

Left: Nutclough Mill after 1884. (PHDA-PNH00510) Right: Nutclough Mill, c.1916. (PHDA-CWS00147) The drawing and the photograph illustrate how the mill grew in size, with the addition of the tower and the additional range to the right, and also how terraces, all 'top and bottom' in layout, now crowd the valley immediately behind.

The 'cutting' (a term especially appropriate in this case) indicates the risks fustian cutters faced handling a sharp knife on a day-to-day basis. It could be one reason why Virgil later switched to a retail role.

It may be no surprise that Virgil moved away from Hebden Bridge. It was his younger brother, Crossley, who, as Andrew Bibby recounts, became a key figure at the Fustian Co-operative.

In the 1891 census Virgil is listed as living with his family in Briercliffe, a village three miles outside Burnley[6] and managing a 'tailor and outfitters' shop'. He was working for Joseph Spencer, his father-in-law, managing Joseph's Burnley business, a position he still held in 1895. (See page 63)

By 1901 he had moved away from the clothing business. The census lists him as a poultry farmer. In 1911 as an 'egg and butter factor', a factor being an agent or middleman. The three eldest children had stayed loyal to the mill and are listed as cotton weavers. One of Virgil's sons, William Percy, died of smallpox in what had been German East Africa in 1918, after three and a half years' service in the RAMC as an ambulance driver. His cousin, Reginald, Joseph Spencer's fourth son, had been killed at Arras the previous year.[7] Virgil died in 1921.

11

Cottonopolis

'Manchester, like a diligent spider, is placed in the centre of the web, and sends forth roads and railways towards its auxiliaries, formerly villages, but now towns, which serve as outposts to the grand centre of industry.'[1]

'Two towns in one'

As we've seen, access to the heart of 'Cottonopolis' was easy. A train ride of less than thirty miles from Hebden Bridge would have taken Joseph to Manchester's Victoria Station, the Manchester terminus of the Lancashire and Yorkshire Railway.

Arriving in Manchester must have been quite an experience. When it had opened in 1844 Victoria's train shed would have been a wonder of the age, 'as large as the nave of many cathedrals'. By 1880 it had competition across the city, with the completion of the Midland Railway's Central Station and its 'spaciously-spanned roof'.[2]

We may wonder how Joseph, with his own business at the age of twenty-seven, responded to a city ('seen through a haze of smoke') on this scale, with its extraordinary energy and self-belief, and still so much a work-in-progress. It was a remarkable place to have on your doorstep. But alongside opportunity lay deprivation, characterised in 1844 by a French visitor, Léon Faucher, as follows:

'There also are two towns in one: in the one portion, there is space, fresh air, and provision for health; and in the other, everything which poisons and abridges existence; the crowding of cottages and families together; dark and gloomy courts, which are both damp and contagious.'[3]

By Joseph's time, Manchester had moved on. It was no longer built 'upon the infinite abysses', in Thomas Carlyle's words[4], but it remained a city of extraordinary contrasts.

Taking a walk

Let's imagine Joseph walking from the station to the heart of the city. I'm taking *Mercantile Manchester*[5], a remarkable overview of late nineteenth-century Manchester, published in 1896, as my guide.

He would have walked via the older areas, around Market Street*, still with 'close-packed brick buildings in courts and alleys', passing 'substantial warehouses ... of massive strength', to buildings 'entirely of stone', and the stone carved 'at first sparingly and later with a freer and even a lavish hand'. Let's assume his destination was the Royal Exchange, 'where is focused in representative forms not only the trade of Manchester, but many of the manufacturing industries of Lancashire'.

Market Street, Manchester, looking east, 1885. (Francis Frith Collection)

Through its portico 'you gain access to the largest room in the world devoted to commercial purposes'. From 'the dense multitude' on the great floor 'comes the confused and intermingling roar of many voices uniting to produce something like the subdued roar of the sea'.

'Hither come spinners and manufacturers from the immediate district and the distant Lancashire towns to meet their customers ...' The spinners sell to the manufacturers and to export brokers, and 'the manufacturers or their agents have come to dispose of their cloth to the merchants, calico printers, or whoever may be interested in dealing with it'. Mixed in are the makers of boilers and spindles and looms, and the bleachers and dyers and printers – and so many others.

'Half past two on a Tuesday and Friday was High 'Change, when 8,000 traders met on the floor and carried out business under the blue domes.'[6]

At one level it was intensely local and Lancashire, at another it was worldwide – in one month, June 1895, almost 20 million pounds of cotton

---

* 'Market Street, now given up mainly to shops and offices, and which, with its crowded footways, and its roadway at times almost congested with trams and vehicular traffic of all kinds, has come to be regarded as one of the famous streets of the world.' On the other side of town was the Palace Theatre, home of popular entertainments such as the Tiller Girls, an act which originated in Manchester in 1889. Whether Joseph ever took time out to watch them is doubtful.

yarn were exported – to as far afield as China and Japan. And almost 480 million yards of cotton piece goods, to China, Turkey, Egypt, Brazil, Argentina ...

Manchester like no other place in the kingdom gave you a perspective on the world.

> Joseph's focus was of course local. But it is worth stepping aside for a moment to take in the consequences of the extraordinary success of Manchester in the nineteenth century for the countries of Empire – above all for India. It was a ruthless trade. What the mills of Lancashire and Europe required was a supply of raw cotton, more than ever important with the onset of the American Civil War. But that meant that the destruction of ancient cotton manufacturing in countries worldwide, notably in its ancient home, India. The loss of manufacturing between 1830 and 1860 amounted to between 2 and 6 million full-time jobs in India alone. No longer with producers able to supply local demand, the market was opened up to manufacturers from Britain and Europe, and above all from Lancashire. In the 1860s the Fielden Brothers of Todmorden (if we can stretch the definition of Lancashire) had so expanded production of cotton goods 'that they began to think about sending cloth for the mass of poor people to Calcutta'. By the end of the century it was reported from Bengal that 'owing to widespread use of European piece-goods ... Indian manufactured goods have gradually disappeared'. Joseph was one very small cog in the vast machine of an Empire both political and commercial. It opened up vast opportunities for manufacturers and merchants in Britain. But at a quite extraordinary cost to others.[7]

Doing business

As a small-town boy Joseph must have been overwhelmed on his first visit, maybe as a young apprentice. His business would have grown with the city. He would have been aware that he was part of something extraordinary, which at the same time became the ordinary, the everyday. Joseph's own ambitions would have been inspired by and grown with the big city.

He may from time to time have had business at the Exchange but his focus from the beginning would have been to establish a core range of contacts, and they would have been the 'home trade houses ... distributed in a radius around the Infirmary, occupying part of Portland Street, York Street, High Street, Church Street and Dale Street ...'

He'd also have been attracted to Deansgate, where later he had his own premises. 'Back in the 1860s Deansgate had been lined with drapers' shops, hosiers, corsetiers, hat and bonnet makers, shoe-makers, spectacle makers, tailors, and, of course, pubs, all of two or three storeys.' The photograph below from 1892 shows how rapidy Manchester had changed.[8]

Deansgate, 1892. (Francis Frith Collection)

The options open to an aspiring merchant tailor would have been legion. His task would be to match the extraordinary variety to the immediate opportunities – what would his customers buy, and with what new ranges could he tempt them? *Mercantile Manchester* gives a good idea of what those ranges were.

'In its early stages this Manchester trade was predominantly a "heavy" one, consisting mainly of piece goods into which cotton entered largely in the form of fustians, calicoes in the grey, bleached, dyed or printed conditions, together with muslins and coloured goods of the gingham kind. Allied to these were linens, woollen cloths and worsted fabrics, and, among purely local manufactures, flannels, silks and smallwares. As the department system grew room was made for fancies, "among which ribbons, laces, furs, feathers, hosiery, gloves and numerous other productions, foreign or native, found place".'

Joseph would have got to know the warehouses well, and he'd have been taken up, maybe, to their upper reaches where he might have found 'bulky packs and piles of bleached calicoes, fustians, velveteens … Still higher, you rise to the uppermost floor, where are muslins, curtains, Turkey twills, table covers, and covering a large space, printed calicoes, satteens, cretonnes, Oxford shirtings and flannelettes.'

Placing orders

How might someone like Joseph put his order together? *Mercantile Manchester* takes as an example a 'small buyer, wanting twenty articles, [who] would order six from one house, and the remaining fourteen from eight to fourteen others, and would instruct the last to send their goods to the warehouse of the first …' The author has, as an imaginary buyer, one 'Briggs of Bristol'. For Briggs, maybe we can read Joseph Spencer of Hebden Bridge. Saturday it seems was the day for despatching multiple orders such as this.

If Saturday night could be a late night for Mr Briggs, awaiting his order from Manchester, it might also have been a late night for Joseph. It might just explain why he wasn't more involved in the multiple activities of Salem Chapel.

Packaging would also have been a matter of serious concern to Joseph. In what condition would his order arrive? It is interesting to read in *Mercantile Manchester* of another wonder of the time, the hydraulic press. Fabrics were squeezed and 'the pieces grow less and less in their aggregate until the required minimum of size is reached'. The process was powered 'by steam engines, pumps and boilers', but as of 1896 no longer on site because Manchester Corporation had recently laid down hydraulic mains, 'with a pressure of water-power of one thousand pounds to the square inch'.

Once packaged, how were the goods which were destined for Hebden Bridge, and everywhere else, loaded? The stations were hives of activity, and apparent chaos. In gas-lit confusion below the station the wagons would be loaded and unloaded, 'while on the platforms, crowded with merchandise of every description, are men hurrying about with deftly handled trucks loaded or empty, and adding the rattle of rapidly moving wheels upon boarded way to the general babel of conflicting sounds, made up of human voices, the blowing of horns, the grind of wheels upon stony ways, and the tramp of horses' hooves.'

This is a description of the North-Western goods station, but Manchester Victoria, the terminus of the Lancashire and Yorkshire Railway, would have been no different. Think back 130 years, and it might have seemed that all this activity was the future of the world. Maybe some people today feel the same about the Manchester Arena, which occupies part of the old Victoria station site.

A close colleague of Joseph was Tom Smith, who in both the 1891 and 1901 census records is listed as a railway clerk. This seemingly humble occupation was crucial to a business such as Joseph's. Tight-packed bundles would arrive at the Hebden Bridge station, and need to be carted the short distance to the store. There was no motor traffic, of course. The Goods Shed which lay between the station and the river was a substantial building.

Alongside the great railway stations and the warehouses and the new town hall, another very impressive series of buildings marked the Manchester landscape. They were the banks. The bank would have been another frequent port of call for Joseph. Which one, we can't say, but the Manchester and Liverpool District Bank had a branch in Hebden Bridge at an early stage, so it would be a strong candidate.

12

Game Changers

Back in his shop Joseph would be dealing with the day to day. He would be taking orders, cutting cloth and making up garments. He would be in his office, dealing with suppliers, placing orders, keeping the show on the road – and planning his next move.

For talking to customers and placing orders he could rely on the mail and the telegraph. The telephone in the last decade of the century will have radically changed the way he talked to suppliers. He was connected with the world.

If the telephone was the late-century game changer, in the early century it had been the railway. Goods-in and goods-out – it's easy to think that it could be taken for granted. But it hadn't always been so.

'The worst-managed in the kingdom …'

The Lancashire and Yorkshire Railway Company ran the line and they didn't have the best reputation. 'The worst-managed in the kingdom and there is neither punctuality civility or cleanliness to be had in travelling in it' was how it was described at a shareholders' meeting in 1878. The shareholders didn't like big increases in capital expenditure, 'particularly in building large lumbering stations'.*

New locomotives, new rolling stock, new stations and goods facilities – all were needed. Improvements came but they came slowly. The year 1878 saw a doubling of the size of the old goods shed and extended sidings to the west of the station. A 'second two-storey bay was added to the warehouse' in 1884. But you sense it was an ongoing struggle. It was 1892 before Hebden Bridge got its new station, 'remarkably close to what we see outwardly today'. [1]

---

* Employees of the carriage and wagon department of the Lancashire and Yorkshire Railway at Newton Heath depot were putting down their own marker for the future. In that same year, 1878, they formed the Newton Heath LYR Football Club. They dropped the 'LYR' from their name in 1892 and in 1902 the club took on the new name of Manchester United.

'This wonderful invention'

The excitement, and the future, as they well knew at the time, lay with the telephone.

Manchester's Royal Exchange contained 'an Exchange within an Exchange', where some 4,000 or more wires, gathered in cables and extending from 'high roof-places over a wider area of the city', were eventually 'centralised within an uppermost chamber or switch room, otherwise known as a Telephonic Exchange'. Manchester was connected *as a city*, but a portion of the room was devoted 'to the conveyance of distant messages, which are carried along "trunk" wires ... connecting Manchester with London, Leeds, Birmingham, or other like remote places'.[2]

'An Exchange within an Exchange ... otherwise known as a Telephonic Exchange.' (Reproduced from Mercantile Manchester)

The author of *Mercantile Manchester* was writing about, and looking back from, the year 1896. Hebden Bridge would have been one of those 'remote places'. The National Telephone Company had been formed in 1881, and Yorkshire was one of its original territories. The years that followed were transformative.

The wider public were curious. A social gathering at Hebden Bridge's Salem Sunday School in January 1884 had as its main attraction an electrical exhibition in one of the classrooms. 'The apparatus consisted of microphones, telephones and telephone transmitters of various forms ...'[3] And telephone poles and wires were another way in which the landscape was changing. The Lancashire and Cheshire Telephone Company 'applied for planning permission to erect telephone poles along the Burnley Road' in February 1888.[4] That same year it was a telephone call that alerted the Todmorden fire brigade to the big fire at Foster Mill.[5] In October 1890, R. S. Blackburn, an electrical engineer, was advertising 'Telephones – lines erected and maintained' as one of the services offered.[6]

William Barker Clothing Co. (Hebden Bridge 1205) and the Hebden Bridge Iron Works were just two companies to have installed telephones at an early stage, probably before 1890. Domestic phones for most people lay in the future but a November 1894 audience at the Hope Street schoolroom were 'very attentive, and seemed extremely anxious to understand the mechanism of this wonderful invention'. (The fact that the lecturer had a 'very weak voice' may have in part explained the close attention.)[7]

I've yet to find any evidence that Joseph Spencer had a telephone installed at his Market Street premises. Suffice it to say, it is very likely that he did. Conversations would have been rudimentary compared to modern times. Negotiating and haggling over prices were still best done face to face. But checking shipments and due dates, and chasing late payments, were areas that would have been greatly facilitated. A telephone would also have lent prestige.

Mail and telegraph

Talk of the telephone gives a sense of the excitement of the time. But Joseph would have built his business using the mail and the telegraph. The telegraph companies were nationalised in 1870 establishing a national network. *White's Directory* from 1870 has the following:

'Post and Money Order and Telegraph Office, and Postal Savings Bank, at Mr Thomas Crawshaw's. Letters are despatched to Manchester at 12.15, 7.15 and 9.20 p.m.; to Halifax at 11.15 a.m.; and to Todmorden at 2.30.' What is immediately striking is the number of despatches to Manchester, three, as compared to Halifax's one. Also, the timing: two were evening, one as late as 9.20. Businesses and mills worked late, and the trains ran late.

An article in the *Hebden Bridge Times* refers to post office premises 'at the junction of Old Gate and Market Street', the tenancy of this building beginning in 1885.

The post office would handle small parcels. The bigger companies would have their own means of transporting bulk goods to and from the station. But for smaller businesses like Joseph's, for wholesale clothiers and small manufacturers, it would have been more of a problem.

'The Hebden Bridge Commercial Association ... wanted a parcels van. Following a deputation to the L&YR, a van and a horse were promised and first the van and then the horse duly arrived in May 1890.'[8] If you had a parcel to be collected you would put a notice in a prominent window for the van to collect as it followed its regular route.

'L&YR [Lancashire and Yorkshire Railway] Parcels & Luggage Collection & Delivery Van N0. 130' at the junction of Albert Street and New Road, Hebden Bridge, c.1900. The boy, probably aged no more than thirteen, would have already been in full-time employment.
(PHDA-GEE00104)

13

All The News

The world changed radically in the thirty years to 1900. Not so the local newspapers. There's something almost reassuring about the continuity they represent. This was a world that was changing by the day but the way it was reported stayed the same.

The local papers were the *Todmorden Advertiser and Hebden Bridge Newsletter* (TAHBN) and the *Todmorden & District News* (TDN). The emphasis on 'district' became more and more marked as the years passed. Also widely read was the *Hebden Bridge Times and Calder Valley Gazette*, founded in 1882, but this has yet to be digitised, and so can't be so easily searched. Joseph may also have read a trade newspaper, the *Cotton Factory Times*. Launched in 1885, and featuring 'voices from the spindle and the loom', by the early 1900s it claimed to sell 53,000 copies an issue.[1] In 1889 a new sister paper, the *Yorkshire Factory Times*, appeared.

Advertising

Joseph Spencer appeared in the local press on multiple occasions over the period between 1874, when he would have been coming up to twenty years old, and 1901, when the family left Hebden Bridge. From 1882 there were the regular display advertisements he placed for his business (initially alongside John Kershaw and Sons, the company to which he'd been apprenticed), always in a standard format, varying a little over the years as he introduced new lines in response to changing demand and fashions. Sourcing his product in Manchester as well as locally he would probably have been ahead of the game in terms of current fashions, and the advertisements suggest that introducing new styles and novelties was very much part of his business plan.

'An alarming explosion'

The business occasionally appeared in the press for other, on occasion more dramatic, reasons.

'23rd February 1894 GAS EXPLOSION – On Monday, at noon, an alarming explosion took place at the shop of Mr Joseph Spencer ... while some alterations were going on. An escape of gas was detected, and one of the workmen, a plumber, went in search of the leak with a lighted candle, and ... a loud explosion took place. A large piece of lead piping as well as part of the woodwork over the window was blown into the street. The report was heard a long distance away.'[2]

There is also an intriguing press cutting from ten years later, September 1904, when Joseph sent a letter to the local gas board, asking about the price of gas for heating a tailor's rooms. It seems a special rate applied. As a one-off request, recorded in a report of the gas board's monthly meeting, this is a curiosity. But it does emphasise the importance of gas as a source of power, and gives a hint of what working conditions must have been like on dark and winter days.[3] By this time Joseph and Emily had left Hebden Bridge and were living in Cheshire. Thomas Spencer was managing the Hebden Bridge store and it is possible that he submitted the request on his father's behalf.

Keen readers of the local papers would have also noticed Joseph's name when he took non-payers to court. In one case the accused's children had ordered a suit. The family had taken delivery but the father had refused to pay. Joseph won, and debts were paid off, as they were in all the cases reported in the press.[4]

One report appeared in a different paper. The *Burnley Express* of 9th January 1895 reported a theft from Joseph's Burnley shop of three overcoats belonging to Joseph and two colleagues. 'Virgil Greenwood, manager for Joseph Spencer, ... said he missed the coat about six o'clock and he heard a man's voice say, "Now's your chance", and heard the coat being torn from the hook.'[5]

Tucked away in a long list of expenses incurred by the Hebden Bridge Local Board, in April 1892, is a reference to lamplighters' overcoats: Joseph had charged 3/- for altering a single overcoat. This was a small sum compared with other items listed either side, which included £7 5s 6d for sett stones, 19/6 for coal, and for 'gas for public lamps £21 17s 6d'.

A report to the Highways Committee in 1893 mentioned that 'the lamplighters' overcoats ordered from Mr Joseph Spencer [had] not yet [been] delivered'. No reason is given for the delay. The lamplighter was a significant civic role, and they'd have needed their overcoats.[6]

Joseph would have been in his thirties, and still too young, and working much too hard, to put himself forward for any of the local town committees. But his name does appear in a report on the activities of the Highway and Nuisance Committee[7], when in 1895 they recommended his plans for his new Birchcliffe Road house should be passed.

Not all news is good

Two years earlier the committee had called in the 'Nuisance Inspector' when reports reached them that 'waste paper' relating to Joseph's business had found its way into the Hebden river.[8] That was literally a ripple in an otherwise smooth flow.

Mentions after 1900 were more serious, and more downbeat, as we will see, relating to the sale of the house on Birchcliffe Road, the family's departure from the town, and the liquidation of the business in 1907.[9]

14

Epidemic

Gas explosions, lamplighters' coats, waste paper in the river – these are reminders of everyday life. It was not, if you looked below the surface, at all rosy.

At some point in the 1880s the family moved from their Market Street address to Brunswick Terrace, according to the electoral register, just north of Market Street. They were in the midst of a hive of activity. Mills were being extended and new houses built. There would have been, for many, a mood of optimism. But there were also big problems. The town was expanding faster than its housing and sanitation could cope.

'Enteric fever'

The 1848 Buildings Act had focused on drainage and toilets, stipulated how plans for houses and streets should be handled, and established local boards of health. Sewers, cleaning streets and slaughterhouses were all included in their remit. Almost all major towns issued byelaws, and new model byelaws were issued in 1877 ... 'largely elaborate details about drainage'.[1] Speculators and landlords, it was hoped, would be brought into line. A healthy workforce was in everyone's interest.*

But the pattern of working-class housing remained the same. In Halifax and Leeds 65 per cent of housing in the 1880s was still being built as back-to-backs. There was improvement in one Halifax development where 'toilets were placed inside the house, but they were only accessible from the outside'.[2]

Hebden Bridge was no better. A government inspector had heard evidence about conditions in the town in 1873. 'We do at Hebden Bridge, as elsewhere, put everything in the river.' On Garden Street, a local resident, Martha Sutcliffe 'spoke of 23 houses served by 3 privies, but 2 are locked and restricted'. There had been twenty-three cases of typhoid in Foster Mill Lane in 1871, eleven in 1872.

---

* Or almost everyone's. A memorandum from the architects' professional body the RIBA, in the 1890s, shows that there could be dissent: they objected to 'new demands for light and air at the back of houses, as rights in these matters partake of "the nature of private property"'.

The report on an outbreak of 'enteric fever' in Hebden Bridge released by the Local Government Board in 1885 showed that the situation had if anything got worse, a direct consequence of the town's rapid growth within a confined area. Housing, within which sanitation had always been poor, simply couldn't keep up.

Enteric fever is typhoid, caused by a specific form of salmonella. It is typically spread through water contaminated with faeces and urine. According to the report, 'it took epidemic form in the autumn of 1884'.

The root causes of the crisis could not be resolved quickly. Councillor Marshall in his address to the Wesleyans in 1890 (see page 72), some five years later, referred to 'ongoing sanitation issues in the town'. They were finally put to rest when, after a sale of land in 1895 and work commissioned in 1899, the new sewage works for Hebden Bridge opened at Redacre in Mytholmroyd in October 1900.

Privies, pails and soil pipes

The report from 1885 is looking for causes and in pursuit of them goes into great detail. 'The habitations are, most of them, labourers' cottages. Building land is costly, and the demand ... is in excess of supply.' Space was cramped.* Cottages 'on the flat ... are built, many of them, back to back'. They had no through ventilation. Most of the rest were four-storey structures, top and bottom houses, Hebden Bridge's unique response to the challenge of building on steep hillsides. Their 'lower tenements' had back walls built into the hillsides with 'no provision made either for drainage between the back wall and the hillside, or for through ventilation'. They were also sadly deficient in light. Cellars were in many cases 'but slightly above the level of the sewers into which they drain'.

'The privy accommodation for older cottages is afforded in several cases by old midden privies' and for new cottages 'by either water closets or pail closets'. Most of the old water closets were flushed by cisterns supplied by springs on the hillside above: 'this supply generally runs short in summer and the closets are then not properly flushed'.

Rain pipes flushed directly into the sewers and the combined effluent fed into the river. The sewers of Todmorden also discharged directly into the Calder, which 'is thus greatly polluted, and when it is low, as it is in the summer, the stench arising from it is much complained of'.

---

* 'One small cottage ... with three small bedrooms has seven, at times nine, occupants while one bedroom is occupied by a patient suffering from typhoid fever.'

Buttress Brink: built in 1851 against a steep hillside with a yard behind which gave access to a second storey, and further steps up to the third and fourth storeys, fifteen small flats housing more than seventy people. (PHDA-WSC00176)

The content of the pails was 'collected by an iron cart ... at night twice a week', a process described as 'scavenging'. The tubs and pails were emptied and replaced without any cleaning. After being mixed with shoddy* from the cotton mills the content was discharged onto land a mile or so away from the town.

One great plus was the availability of water 'from the Local Board waterworks', at Widdop. 'It is far removed from ordinary sources of pollution.' The water 'is laid on in nearly every street, and every facility is given to owners of property to obtain it'. Springs, 'which issue in great numbers from the hillside', were the other source of supply. There was 'generally a most careless disregard of the liability to pollution, from privy pits, slop streamlets, manure piled ... over the land, and from leaking stone sewers'. The report examines each of the main sources of spring supply, from Bridge Lanes at the west end of town, by way of Royd Terrace and Foster Mill, to Birchcliffe to the east. 'The Birchcliffe water is open to pollution on every side.' The report traces the majority of the 1884 cases back to the Birchcliffe supply.

---

* See Appendix Five – types of cloth.

The inspector eliminated milk as a source of infection, though the dairymen were unregistered and 'the cow-houses visited very dark, low in the roof and badly ventilated'. The slaughterhouses on the other hand were 'registered and kept cleanly'.

It is a bleak picture, summed up graphically as follows: 'The facts present themselves in all their fever-abetting reality. Overcrowding, defective ventilation, habitations drawing sewer air through sink-pipes, through soil-pipes, and from filth-sodden soil, water open to pollution on every side ...'

There had been outbreaks of fever at irregular intervals in earlier years but that of 1884 was altogether more serious. 'There is no public means of isolating cases,' the report highlights, 'and no disinfecting apparatus.' (The report compares enteric fever and smallpox patients: the latter were sent away to Halifax and no deaths had been recorded from smallpox in recent years.)

In emphasising waterborne pollution the report avoids any suggestion that old ideas about the 'miasma', foul air deriving from waste matter, as the primary carrier of infections such as typhoid and cholera, rather than water, still held sway with the authors. Lessons had been learnt (albeit slowly) from Edwin Chadwick's reforms to the sewage system in London in the late 1840s whereby sewage had been diverted directly into the Thames. The aim had been to clean the air rather than the water. Cholera outbreaks had continued and the stench from the Thames was awful. The remarkable sewage system introduced by Joseph Bazalgette, which channelled sewage away from London, removed that problem.

There could be no such final solution for Hebden Bridge, and no end to smells from the river, until all sewage could be directed down to, and treated at, an efficient sewage works and that in 1885 still lay fifteen years into the future in 1900. They were major undertakings. The Hebden Bridge sewage works opened in 1900. The Todmorden sewage works, situated by the Calder above Hebden Bridge, was not finally opened until 1908.[3]

Birth and death

A letter which accompanied the report called for the Hebden Bridge Local Board to give the matter its immediate attention. Three of the nine members of the board were Joseph Spencer's relatives by marriage: Handel Halstead, Eli Fielding and Joseph Greenwood. How to respond in the short term to issues which were embedded in the very structure of the town would have been for them, and for everyone in the town, the subject of much discussion. How best to 'secure the efficient ventilation of sewers', to do away with 'old-fashioned midden privies'. The report insisted that hospital accommodation should be provided so as to promptly isolate cases that arise. And existing byelaws should be enforced.

The report also provides what it describes as vital statistics of the Hebden Bridge Urban Sanitary District. Of that immediate area (other population figures cover a wider area) the population in 1871 numbered 4,500, rising to 5,008 in 1881. The average number of births per annum was 155, the number of deaths 105. 'The deaths of children under one year average 25 per annum, at a rate of 161.7 per 1,000 births … The high rate of infant mortality is ascribed … to the lack of mothers' milk, the mothers being themselves engaged in factories …'

15

Home Affairs

When the opportunity arose, probably in 1890, the family moved away from the heart of the town, out west, to Mytholm, about a half-mile's walk from Market Street. (See page 97.) Heath House had been built by the Crowthers, two brothers, Joseph and John, who we met earlier. The Crowthers and Spencers were family friends with a strong Salem Chapel connection. There were two houses within the one building. Joseph Crowther had died young in 1875 and one house would have been vacant. The house had a quiet hillside location with views east and south across the valley. Sanitation would have been one very good reason for their move away from Brunswick Terrace. Emily's brother, the local doctor, would surely have encouraged the move.

A Tyrolean bazaar

Reports on the harsh realities of life are part of the story, but so too are the many upbeat reports on the town's business, religious and social activities. They suggest that Joseph and Emily, and their family, enjoyed an active social life, carried on mainly through Salem Chapel. It is clear that the chapel was a thriving institution, the services well attended, the Sunday school by modern standards extraordinarily so.

Social life and fundraising went hand in hand and never more so than in the countrywide enthusiasm for the bazaar, or in more prosaic terms, a 'sale of work'. One splendid local example is an event at Salem Chapel described at length in the *Todmorden & District News* of 7th October 1887, under the heading 'Tyrolean Bazaar at Hebden-Bridge', with the subhead 'Magnificent Spectacle'. An extraordinary amount of organising must have been involved, and much of this would have fallen on the ladies who in these newly prosperous times were no longer expected to work. The Wesleyans had only moved into their new chapel in 1885, and as the report suggests, they had not lost that all-important fundraising instinct:

'Within a short space of time, the friends connected with the Wesleyan chapel, Hebden Bridge, have raised between three and four thousand pounds for various purposes connected with their sanctuary, and yet they have the courage to enter upon another scheme for clearing their beautiful premises from an incubus and to place an organ in the chapel ... The style of the bazaar is Tyrolean, and represents a Swiss village, and the effect is most charming and realistic. ['Incubus', being a rather unpleasant demon, is a happy moment of journalistic licence. Turning in lively reports on endless social events can't have been easy.]

'It is held in the large school-room. On entering the room the visitor is introduced apparently into the very heart of an Alpine village ... On either side are chalets ... the end of the village is bounded by a rushing mountain torrent, behind which is a stretch of Alpine scenery, beautifully painted ... The maidens, matrons and gentlemen who are in attendance on the visitors are attired in characteristic costume. The ladies wear black cheminettes ... no wonder some of them succeed in inducing young men to part so freely with their coin. The gentlemen were attired in black velvet knee breeches, and red stockings ...'

Each chalet had attendants, and the great and the good of the chapel all seem to have been in attendance. Mrs Spencer was one of a number of ladies 'in attendance on the Berne chalet'. Mr Joseph Spencer's chalet was Tell's cottage, described as 'the young men's stall'. Joseph would have been thirty-three, Emily thirty-two years old.

The report doesn't tell us why a Tyrolean scene was chosen. The first guided tour of the Alps, organised by Thomas Cook, had taken place in 1863. The publication of *Heidi* in 1881, in English translation in 1882, may have further encouraged the craze for Swiss and by association Tyrolean scenes among the English – and Calder Valley – public.*

It's also interesting for the long list of the names of participants, many of which recur in other reports on Salem activities in subsequent years. These included the Horsfall, Smith, Fielding and Pickles families.

As late as October 1909 the chapel were still holding Tyrolean bazaars, this time to pay for organ refurbishments. Stallholders 'were dressed in Swiss fancy costume'. 'Tyrol' remained a catch-all term for the Alps.

'The ladies have exerted themselves'

For any activity at Salem Chapel there was always a minister on hand, and in the case of a 'sale of work' on New Year's Day 1890 no fewer than three. Before the event began 'the Rev. Geo. Oyston gave out a hymn ... the Rev.

---

* The craze may be traced back to Albert Smith's 1853 London show, *The Ascent of Mont Blanc*. It was 'replete with ushers in dirndls ... a cut-out Swiss chalet, dioramas of the mountain ...', as described in Robert Macfarlane's *Mountains of the Mind*. The show ran for six years.

J. Hubbard read the 90th Psalm, and the Rev. G. Quiggin offered prayers'.

This was an event in which Emily Spencer was very much involved. She has all too few mentions in the local press, and she is of course always 'Mrs Joseph Spencer'. Sales of work were frequent events and this particular one was organised 'by the energetic friends connected with Salem Wesleyan Chapel'. Their intention was to raise about £300 toward 'upholstering and decorating their fine and commodious chapel'.

'The ladies have exerted themselves,' read the report[1], 'in such a manner as to merit unbounded praise; they have been plying the needle with great dexterity for a number of months, both at home and in the sewing meetings.'

The stalls 'were of the Gothic type and beautifully draped in Japanese art muslin and pink and blue sateen ...' The young men's stall 'displayed a choice variety of objects, including glass ware, Parian marble and bronze ornaments ... clocks, barometers', and much else.

I wonder if they might have been happier playing football, currently undergoing a remarkable upsurge across the north of England.

One group of ladies ran a fancy stall. Another was run by members of the sewing class, one of whom was Mrs Joseph Spencer. This was 'laden with ladies' and children's underclothing and household linen, in addition to a few ornamental items'. The sewing class may have been something of an institution among the Salem ladies.

The afternoon and evening were 'enlivened' by a string band from Todmorden. 'In the lower rooms several entertainments were given.' One room was devoted to statuary of biblical figures, best understood in modern terms as tableaux vivants, 'living pictures', where scenes from the Bible had long been popular. 'The representations were very good.' Providing a contrast in another room was 'a faithful representation of Jumbo ... which moved about upon a stage'. This probably took the form of a magic lantern show, or diorama. The contrast between stillness and simple movements, in the period immediately before moving pictures, made for a popular entertainment.

Jumbo apart, God was never too far removed from proceedings. Nor indeed was the everyday world, as a speech by a Councillor Marshall of Todmorden, who had been invited to open proceedings, reminded them.

'He remembered coming to Hebden-bridge a long time ago, when the place was nothing but a large village, but had now grown to a place of considerable importance ... and established a wide reputation with regard to their staple trade.'

He also 'wished to congratulate them on another matter ... Their town was in a fairly healthy condition.' (No more, it seems, than 'fairly healthy'.)

'He understood they were seeking to extend their borders and if that was granted he hoped that they would devote their attention to sanitary matters … and that they would remedy the sanitary evils that had brought so much distress to so many families.'

It's evident the Wesleyans of Hebden Bridge knew how to let their hair down, and they were an imaginative and creative bunch. Who needs alcohol, they might have said, to have fun. At the same time, there is an earnestness about proceedings.

Fundraising for 'upholstering the chapel' had in this case been the end in view. Fundraising for missions, home and overseas, was a more serious business, with which as we will see Joseph was very much involved. Another occasion which had over centuries brought people together had been an annual dole to the local poor. How long this survived changing times, and the strictures of the new Poor Law, I can't say but it was still something which engaged members of Salem Chapel back in the 1860s. A Halifax Courier report refers to a 'Wesleyan annual dole of linen goods, consisting of shirts and underclothing, &c., to the poorer families in the neighbourhood'. One common denominator of all such occasions was that they took place under the watchful eye of the local minister. Should they want to escape, how might they have done so?[2]

Escaping the minister's eye

One place to have done so could have been the unlikely settings of floral and agricultural shows which were very much part of valley life. (The Hebden Bridge Floral and Agricultural Society had been founded in 1880.) I've a sense that Joseph and Emily and their two young children are relaxing, and having fun, at just such a show in August 1883.[3] A performance by the Heptonstall Brass Band was a highlight. And there's a suggestion of an interest in fruit and vegetables in the reference to a prize of 2/6d for the best six dessert apples 'given by Joseph Spencer, tailor and woollen draper'.

There are other later references to horticultural prizes presented by the Spencers, and one as late as 1903. A report on the Hebden Bridge and Calder Valley Agricultural Show in the *Todmorden & District News* of 8th May refers to 'a prize of £2 10s and hat presented by Mr Joseph Spencer, Market Street' for the 'best cow in milk, three years and upwards'. What kind of hat it was is not divulged. It was a big show, and there was an abundance of prizes.

Joseph and family had already left Hebden Bridge, but the shop of course remained, and the prize was offered by the business and not Joseph personally – maybe the idea came from Joseph's son, Thomas, now acting as manager.

'Louie Fuller's skirt dance ...'

I mentioned earlier the interest in demonstrations of the telephone. More exciting would have been the cinematograph, which 'synchronised' photographs and phonograph recordings, and as part of a programme at the Co-operative Hall in 1898 featured 'the Jubilee Procession in London, haunted castle, snowballing, Louie Fuller's skirt dance ...' and more.[4]

A short train journey away, in Halifax, were several theatres, including the Theatre Royal and the Grand Theatre. Did the family ever venture that far? For music hall, for Joseph and Emily, maybe, and for a pantomime for the children, more than likely.

An announcement in the Halifax Courier in November 1896 had a fine line in superlatives. 'LITTLE PATTI, the Vocal Wonder' was 'the Greatest Child Operatic Vocalist Living'. 'Miss BELL DINMOST' was 'the Greatest of all Burlesque Actresses and Low Comedy Turns'.[5]

'Popular Townsman, ARTHUR BINGLEY' brought everyone gently down to earth with 'a budget of new songs and old favourites.' Only for extravagance to re-appear with 'PAUL'S ORIGINAL THEATOGRAPH', 'Engaged at enormous salary from the Athenaeum, London', and offering 'Living Pictures' and 'Marvellous Animated Photographs'.

Later that same month they had more 'Animated Photographs', combined with music hall and an intriguing sketch described as 'A Trilby Muddle'.

And, moving on a few years, to the early 1900s, *Aladdin* was the big Christmas pantomime at the Grand Theatre. A later Milton Ray production, *The Girl from Japan*, in 1904, starred a Miss Madie Scott and it's possible she played Aladdin in this production. She is described as a music hall comedienne, 'delightfully dainty and demure ... [Her] marked originality, graceful and artistic movements proclaim her as an artiste of high attainments.'6

Poster for a pantomime at the Grand Theatre, Halifax, c.1901. (Mary Evans Picture Library)

'... the largest show in the entire World'

For maybe the most popular entertainment of all there was no need to take the train. Sanger's Circus came to the town, and it was, it seems, a regular visitor. 'This renowned circus', reported the *Todmorden Advertiser and Hebden Bridge Newsletter* in May 1882[7], 'visited Hebden Bridge on Friday last, the tent being pitched in the field formerly tenanted by the cricket club. The procession of the large stud of horses and gaily dressed equestrians was much admired by large numbers of people as it passed through the principal streets of the town at noon.'

It returned in April 1888[8] when it advertised itself as 'the largest show in the entire World ... three rings all going at the same time ... monkeys, ostriches, camels, llamas ... a band of musical elephants ... seats for 10,000 people'. The circus procession was described as 'two solid miles of oriental magnificence'.

The American West was also well represented. 'Colonel Leglere, the Buffalo Hunter, will introduce scenes of Rocky Mountain Life, Cowboys and Indians ... the Redwood Stage Coach Robbery ... all the habits and customs of life in the Western Wild Prairies.'

I assume Joseph would have allowed his staff a few minutes respite to watch the procession pass along Market Street. For mill workers, how long hours at the loom squared with Friday afternoon performances I can't say.

The town also of course made its own entertainment. The annual carnival was an occasion for a procession of carriages and floats through crowd-lined streets decorated with flags and bunting, with brass bands very much in evidence.[9]

Circus parade in Hebden Bridge, 1897. To the left is the Co-op building and in the far distance the White Horse Hotel. (PHDA-ALC05005)

*

I've looked in vain for any mention of Joseph's name, or indeed Thomas's, in connection with the extraordinary growth in football and cricket either side of 1890, and with new leagues and rapid growth in club memberships. Much of Saturday would be spent working in the business and Sunday was chapel. Chapel could take up evenings as well.

In the end, maybe there was no escape from the minister's eye, and indeed the minister, as is amply demonstrated by the Spencer family photo album from the period, which includes two men of the cloth. The local minister from Salem Chapel was installed just four doors away on Birchcliffe Road. And Thomas Spencer had of course been educated at a school originally founded to train young Wesleyan ministers.

Two local ministers, assumed to be Wesleyan, as yet unidentified.

16

Chapel and Choir

'Remember how short thy time is'

Big sums of money needed to be raised to equip a chapel such as Salem which, like Birchcliffe Baptist Chapel, was built to impress the neighbours as well as to glorify God. Joseph and his wider family were very much involved.

Left: Salem Wesleyan Chapel, opened 1885 (photograph from 1910). Capacity 1,050 people. (PHDA-ALC06329)

Right: Birchcliffe Baptist Chapel, opened 1898. In the unofficial competition between chapels for the grandest edifice the Birchcliffe Baptists, aided by an elevated position, albeit a little out of town, were clear winners. (PHDA-ALC05182)

The Trustees responsible for the building of a new manse[1], completed in 1870, included James Kershaw and Thomas Walton.* James Kershaw was a principal subscriber, along with Thomas Smith, who may have been the father of Joseph's friend, Tom Smith. They also feature on the building committee for the new Sunday school, opened in 1874, along with Joseph's brother-in-law Eli Fielding.

---

* Thomas Walton and James Kershaw also appear together in a very different guise, as agents for Scottish Union, and The National Boiler Insurance Co. Ltd. They may have found it a lucrative diversion. Boilers were more than relevant for Thomas Walton as manager at Foster Mill.[2]

The Trustees brought together in 1884 to form a building committee for the new chapel included Eli Fielding, and this time Joseph Spencer also featured. 'Remember how short thy time is,' a verse from Psalm 80, was the text of the last sermon given in the old chapel. When the trust was renewed the following year Joseph was no longer on the list (a neat irony, given the sermon text), but James Kershaw had re-appeared.

The mighty new organ inaugurated in 1888 also required major investment. Further fundraising was required for its refurbishment in 1909.

Salem Chapel's new organ was a mighty affair, dominating even the raised and centred pulpit, which was itself meant to symbolise the primacy of God's word, as spoken by the preacher. Could it be that 'song' in the service of God ranked even higher? (Reproduced from Dickenson, History of Salem Chapel)

'… born in song'

The organ needed a choir.* Sermons do not normally stand the test of time. Unless they're Martin Luther King, maybe never. Choirs and congregational singing live on long in the memory. The old *Methodist Hymn Book* began with the words, 'Methodism was born in song.' Some might argue it was born in John Wesley's sermons. But it is arguably more for his brother, Charles's hymns that the Wesleys are remembered today.

Local author, Colin Spencer, mentions the practice of the girls working at their sewing machines 'either side of a long narrow table', singing as they worked. 'Most were members of a choir at church or chapel and they sang hymns and the popular songs of the day.' [3]

The choir at Salem Chapel was, in the 1890s, conducted by Joseph's business associate and friend, Tom Smith. They would have practised hymns and anthems, one such being 'Not unto us, O Lord', sung to celebrate of the anniversary of the local branch of the Wesleyan Foreign Mission. Rehearsals may have been, but performances were not, occasions for levity.

---

* Or the choir needed an organ. Organs were a feature of Anglican worship and initially strongly resisted by the Nonconformist chapels. But by mid-century attitudes were changing to the extent that they became in the absence of stained-glass east windows the dominant feature, rising high, as we've seen, behind the preacher's head.

Tom Smith.   Clara Smith.

But we cannot be certain. Reports of a February 1898 'tea and entertainment' in aid of the new Birchcliffe Baptist Chapel suggest the Baptists at least knew how to have a little fun. 'Songs were contributed by Mr J. M. Wilcock, "Last of the Boys", Mr G. Helliwell, "Lost Chord", and Mr J. Cockcroft, "The Desert", all of which were very creditably performed. The Rev. J. Gay gave a selection from Shakespeare's *Richard III*, with very good effect.' A 'Tyrolean choir' made up of young ladies sang, among other items, 'I Burst Out Laughing', and 'Stitching Away'.[4]

Choirs were also in competition with each other. The choir from Wainsgate Baptist Chapel, high on the hillside above Hebden Bridge, won the first prize at the national Nonconformist Choirs Festival in 1908.[5]

Away from the Wesleyan chapel Tom Smith was also involved 'in meetings for musical improvement in a room behind the shop occupied by Mr Jas. Kershaw'.[6] The same group also 'indulged at times in dramatic representations'. Joseph knew James well of course, and he would have known the room behind the shop. He may or may not have been persuaded to exercise his voice. We may speculate that Emily Spencer's Wesleyan sewing group also sang, as did the mill girls, as they sewed. They may have been members of the chapel choir.

Close harmony

The Baptists were picking up on a wider enthusiasm for popular singing, and glees, as they were known, in particular. Featuring songs 'sung unaccompanied and in close harmony' glees had a big following, with glee clubs in towns and villages throughout the West Riding, including Todmorden. Their tunes had much in common with Nonconformist hymn tunes.[7]

At the 'public tea and meeting' marking the opening of the new Co-operative premises in 1877 'The Wainsgate Singing Class ... was present to enliven the proceeding with glees, etc ... The chairman first called for the glee, "When Winds Blow Soft", after which he proceeded with his opening address.' The popular song 'Thou Art so Near and Yet so Far' preceded the secretary's report.

There's nothing loud or strident about the choice of music, rather a gentility designed to encourage harmonious proceeding.[8]

17

Good Works

The history of Salem Chapel records 'the practical concern which the Society of Salem had, not only for the spiritual welfare, but also the material ... needs of their neighbours, especially at the time of the Cotton Famine'. It references an article in the *Halifax Courier* of 27th September 1862:

'Many of the inhabitants of the village [as it then was] are practically acquainted with the fact of the effects of the Wesleyan annual dole of linen goods, consisting of shirts and underclothing, etc, to the poorer families of the neighbourhood. This year we understand the gifts are to be of an unprecedented extent. We hear of several gentlemen ... having given liberally ... The goods are made by the Wesleyan Female Sewing Class gratis.'*

There are no later mentions of the 'dole' in the local press. What do get reported are the various chapel gatherings which were consistently well attended.

Christmas Day was always put to good use by the Salem Wesleyans. The morning may have been for family and present-giving but later in the day they staged Christmas teas which, given the numbers involved, would have been for the wider community as well as the Wesleyans. Several such events were reported on at length, the earliest being the tea held on Christmas Day 1873:

'Salem, Wesleyan – On Christmas Day, 450 had tea in Salem Methodist School. The after meeting was held in the chapel, the platform and orchestra being elaborately decorated. The Rev. J. Priestley presided; the secretary, Mr Joseph Spencer, read the report, and spoke in terms of praise of those who were using every exertion to get the new school out of debt. The cost of the new school has been estimated at £3000.'[1]

This suggests a serious turn of mind at a young age. Joseph would have been no more than nineteen. The £3,000 no doubt refers to the new Sunday school formally opened in November 1874. I mentioned earlier that a Wesleyan 'Academy' or day school had been founded in the 1860s. The new premises would no doubt have been used by both the Sunday and the day school.

---

* The men gave 'liberally' of goods made by the women 'gratis'.

In later years the Christmas Day event is described as the 'annual festival'. In 1888 'the tea was served in the schoolroom to well over 400 people ... The Rev. George Oyston occupied the chair ... it was regretted that there had been a slight falling-off in the number of scholars. The year was commenced with 507 on the roll and closed with 504. The number of teachers and officers was put down at 84.' The numbers are impressive.[2]

Messrs Joseph Spencer, George Pickles, F. W. Horsfall and R. Redman were among the those who gave addresses. 'The meeting throughout,' the *Todmorden & District News* reported, 'was of a pleasant and interesting character ...' (Reports on meetings and gatherings are almost always mild and emollient. To be a real news story someone would have to have spoken out of turn ... and it would seem no one ever did.)

Another report from two years later, in 1890, mentions 516 scholars. There were eighty teachers who were also members of the chapel. The chapel had 350 members – people officially received into membership of the Wesleyan community, the equivalent of confirmation. The report adds, 'They had a beautiful organ and a splendid piano, so that they had not only provided for the body and mind but the soul as well.'[3]

'The Demosthenes of early Methodism'

Joseph continued his involvement in both chapel and school. In September 1888 the *Todmorden Advertiser and Hebden Bridge Newsletter* reported that 'a Service of Song, entitled "Uncle Tom", was rendered most pleasingly by the choir... Mr Joseph Spencer, Market Street, presided.' A collection of £3 went to the Sunday school organ fund. 'The attendance was not as good as usual.'[4]

A report from three months earlier refers to the opening of 'the new organ', presided over by the organist of St Patrick's Cathedral, Dublin. It seems the chapel was now aspiring to an organ for the Sunday school as well.[5]

The *Todmorden & District News* of 24th October 1890 reported that Sunday 'throughout the Wesleyan connexion' was Children's Sunday. 'In the school addresses were delivered by Messrs Joseph Spencer, Geo. Pickles, Thomas Midgley and Amos Crossley to the elder portion ...'[6]

There were also visits from itinerant worthies to contend with. This from the *Todmorden & District News* of 5th April 1895:

'On Monday last, the Rev. Dinsdale T. Young, one of the most eloquent preachers and lecturers in the Wesleyan Methodist connexion, paid a visit to Salem Chapel, Hebden-bridge. In the afternoon he preached to a fairly good congregation, and in the evening he delivered a lecture. His subject was "The Demosthenes of early Methodism, or from Cobbler's bench to President's chair". The audience [the report continued] was not so large as the interesting character of the lecturer warranted. The chair was occupied by Mr Joseph Spencer …'[7]

Again, audiences were not always what they might have been. Joseph it seems had both patience and a creditable sense of duty.

Centenary celebration

The centenary of the Sunday school movement, in 1880, was a big event across the nation, and celebrated with great enthusiasm in the town. All the Methodist (Primitive as well as Wesleyan) and Baptist Sunday schools took part. But not the Church of England. The numbers were impressive, with almost 3,500 scholars in all, of which Salem contributed 475. If all, or most, attended it would have been an event celebrated on the hillside rather than the town.

The choir, of adults and scholars, was drilled to follow the exact movements of the baton of the conductor, Mr Kitchen. We might have expected children's hymns, or even song or two. But the programme of music could hardly have been more solemn: psalm tunes and Handel choruses.

It is worth recalling John Wesley's views on children's education, as laid down in *A Plain Account of Christian Perfection*, which he wrote to guide education at the school at Kingswood that he established in the 1750s. 'He that plays when he is a child will play when he is a man.' Also, 'As we have no play-days, the school being taught every day of the year except Sundays, so neither do we allow time for play on any day …'[8]

Mission work

One area of the chapel's activities was of particular interest to Joseph, and that was mission work. He, and his fellow Wesleyans, may well have been inspired by the Forward Movement associated with the Rev. Hugh Price Hughes, founder of the Wesleyan West London Mission. It sought 'to provide centres of evangelism and, at the same time, work for the relief of poverty and distress'.

This led to the building of 'central halls' in many big cities. 'Although primarily places for worship, the halls also offered facilities for wholesome entertainment and provided a wide range of social services. Their purpose-built premises were designed to look quite different from the prevailing Gothic style of conventional churches.'[9] The architects and builder of Hebden Bridge's brand-new Salem Chapel may have been influenced by similar ideas.

As early as February 1885 the *Todmorden Advertiser and Hebden Bridge Newsletter* reported on a juvenile missionary meeting addressed by Joseph. In October 1890 he presided over another juvenile meeting, held as part of the Annual Mission Service. In November 1894 he was reported as chairing a mission meeting in Heptonstall where foreign missions were the focus.

In January 1899 the *Todmorden &and District News* reported on something altogether more ambitious, 'The Wesleyan Million Guinea Challenge'. (That was quite a sum for 1899.) A meeting 'to advocate this scheme' was held at the Cragg Vale Wesleyan Chapel, but the audience 'was only of moderate size'. 'The scheme was spoken to by Rev. C. Denham, Mr J. Horsfall and Mr Jos. Spencer.'

Remarkably the Wesleyans did reach their target. By 1904 the Challenge had raised nearly £1,076,000, money that 'was used to build chapels and schools, and to support overseas mission, temperance work and children's homes, as well as to build Westminster Central Hall in London …'[10]

This was the heyday of Empire, with Queen Victoria's Diamond Jubilee in 1897. Joseph's work, not least his close acquaintance with Manchester, would have given him wide horizons. Mission work, both home and overseas, with India and Africa the primary focus, would have done the same.

Temperance, talks, tea … and trips to the seaside

Wesleyans and alcohol didn't mix. Public teas were as we would expect the rule at chapel and indeed at Co-op gatherings. Elsewhere in the town, working men gathered at the Hole in the Wall pub on Old Gate. Sober men and women throughout the country saw drunkenness as the pre-eminent public enemy. Children's education was part of the solution, and its practical manifestation was the Band of Hope, which became a national movement in 1855, the year of Emily Spencer's birth. By the 1890s it had 2 million young people as members and as many as 10,000 meetings a week across the country. Talks, teas and trips to the seaside were all part of the fun, and we can assume would have been for the Spencer children.

The Band of Hope was more than just a temperance movement, it had the higher aim of a social transformation, 'to facilitate the absorption of upwardly mobile working-class families into respectable society'.[11] Samuel Smiles in his book *Self-help* developed similar ideas. He argued for the better education of working men whose 'pay nights were often a Saturnalia of riot and disorder'.[12] Working men, sober and motivated, could lift themselves out of poverty.

The cause was also taken up by the Nonconformist churches, and became through them part of the ethos of the emerging middle class. Temperance and sobriety were more than spiritual imperatives. They were markers which set them apart from the working class.

With their Band of Hope banner, members of the Cross Lanes Wesleyan Chapel outside the old council offices, and ready, with decorated carriage and bicycles, for a parade.
(PHDA-ALC01448)

Signing the pledge, not to drink alcohol, was something all children were invited to do, a lifelong commitment that not all would have observed. Joseph and Emily's children would have been no exception.

The Hebden Bridge and Heptonstall Temperance Society had been founded as far back as 1852. It evolved in time into the local branch of the Band of Hope. Friday evening, being pay night, may well have been in their minds when the society put up seven candidates in the 1894 local elections with the specific aim of securing the closure of the Hole in the Wall pub. Only one candidate was elected, and the pub stayed open, and was indeed rebuilt in 1899.[13]

It survived until 2012, which could be chalked up as a failure for temperance.

Patrons of the Hole in the Wall pub, 1874. With their tankards, glasses, cups, battered hats and pipes and barrels, they look to be a jaunty and yet innocent crowd. Come Friday evenings, maybe less so. (Jack Uttley Photo Library)

Grocer, publican and (possibly) postman, at Buttress Bottom, c.1900. The pub is the Hole in the Wall, the time, maybe midday, and the landscape looks to be entirely sober at this point. (PHDA-ALC05185)

Temperance marked out a great divide in the town, as in towns and cities throughout the land. Joseph and his family, and their Salem Chapel congregation, knew which side they were on.

18

Relaxing

Home life for Joseph and Emily would have been dominated by children. Just at the age when the first two, Thomas and Lilian, would have required a little less attention, being twelve and ten, they started again, with four arriving over the four years from 1890 to 1894. Their toys are a subject well beyond the scope of this book. As are nursery rhymes, fairy tales and folk tales. But it is worth noting that for older children a range of novels, which are classics to this day, had recently been published. These include *Coral Island* (1857), *The Water Babies* (1863), *Black Beauty* (1877) and of course *Treasure Island* (1883). Robert Louis Stevenson's *Child's Garden of Verses* dates from 1885. Dickens also contributed with *Oliver Twist*. They would have been available initially mainly in middle-class homes but in time libraries were also to make a major contribution.*

Lilian's granddaughter, Barbara, recalls her grandmother later in life owning a grand piano, 'which she would play with accomplishment'. Chopin was part of her repertoire. She would have learnt as a child. Tom Smith, choirmaster at Salem Chapel, a close family friend, may have doubled as a piano teacher. We can imagine Joseph and Emily buying piano scores so they could gather round the piano like any good late Victorian family to play and sing the children's and the popular songs of the time. If they didn't play themselves, at least they had Lilian.

What the popular songs might have included we can only conjecture. The bawdy songs out of music halls such as 'Cushie Butterfield' would have got short shrift. But the sentiments of 'Home Sweet Home' may have appealed. 'Come into the Garden, Maude,' a setting of Tennyson, would soften any heart. 'Annabelle Lee' introduced tragedy into the love story. Hymns, and carols at Christmas, would also have been part of everyday life, at home as well as church.

They would, as good Wesleyans, have been comfortable with the sentiment and sentiments of 'The Lost Chord', as were the Baptists (see page 80). 'The Volunteer Organist' (1893) is a song which would have

---

* Thomas and Lilian were not as soon as age allowed despatched to work in the mills. And Emily could be a full-time mother. They were privileged. And novels were, literally, a novelty.

resonated with regular churchgoers everywhere: 'Our organist is ill today, will someone play instead?/An anxious look crept o'er the face of every person there ...'*

Leisure time was of course something that for most children, 'half-timers', with school for half the day and working in the mills for the second half, and mothers also working long hours, would have been in short supply. For adults those great resources, reading rooms and libraries, were, as we will see, opening up opportunities. Children would have to wait awhile.

Libraries

Most of the larger Sunday schools had lending libraries (see page 19), which in time became a resource for the whole community.[1] The Hebden Bridge Baptists had a library of 1,500 books in 1834, and Heptonstall Slack followed in 1836, adding a Reading and Mental Improvement Society in 1875, 'with a room open two nights a week provided with papers and periodicals'.

But chapel agendas were overtly spiritual and improving. It was the local co-operative societies who responded to (and helped create) the demand for popular literature. Joseph Greenwood was again a leading figure. In 1875 'in a paper read at a conference of Yorkshire co-operatives [he] had argued (against some opposition) for every store to have its own reading room and lending library.'[2]

A reading room 'for the benefit of members' on the second storey of the new Co-operative Hall opened in 1877.[3] Plans from 1890 and 1903 show proposed additions to the reading room. The Liberal Club in Crown Street also had a reading room. But reading rooms, usually only open to men, and with more of a focus on reference, were only part of the story.

Libraries on the other hand were open to both men and women. We have hard evidence for 1889 from the annual report of its librarian to the Industrial Co-operative Society up the road in Todmorden.[4] Fiction, bound magazines, history and biography and voyages and travels were the most popular categories. Religion and theology languished. The total number of books borrowed was almost 20,000.

---

* I well remember my father panicking when, as an occasional pianist, he was asked to play the organ at a local Methodist church, the regular organist being indisposed.

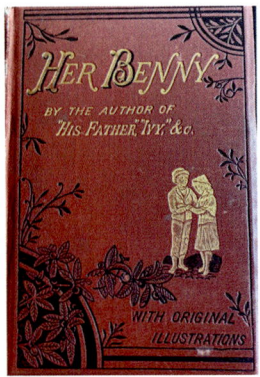 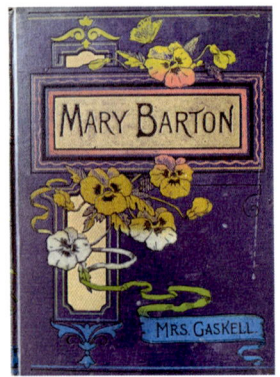

Two contrasting editions of popular titles: Silas K. Hocking's Her Benny, *c.1900, and Mrs Gaskell's* Mary Barton, *with an embossed cover, c.1880.*

The Todmorden library had duplicate sets of the novels by Mrs Worboise, Edna Lyall, S. K. Hocking and Mrs Wood, who were 'most in demand'. Hocking's *Her Benny* is the story of two children in Liverpool sent out to live on the streets. Edna Lyall's first great success was *We Two*, a novel based on the life of the social reformer, Charles Bradlaugh. The legacy of Charles Dickens and Mrs Gaskell lived on, though the binding of the edition of *Mary Barton* shown here may have pushed the price beyond what most libraries were prepared to pay.

Local writers will also have featured, in addition, of course, to the Brontës. One may have been John Hartley, a writer 'well known for his dialect works'. Two of his novels 'not entirely in the vernacular' were *A Rolling Stone: a tale of wrongs and revenge* and *Many a Slip: a domestic romance*. Both novels were published in Wakefield in 1878.[5]

The choice of novels suggests that women were the main borrowers from libraries. That reading rooms were often only accessible to men didn't go unquestioned. The *Hebden Bridge Times* of 20th February 1884 reported that 'at a Women's Co-operative League meeting in the Co-operative Hall attended by about 220 members and sympathisers with the league, "Mr R. Lindley made a few forcible and pointed remarks. He said young men of the present day had plenty of facilities for improving themselves, reading rooms for instance, but very few facilities of the same description were within the reach of young women."'

Thomas Walton, another Thomas Walton, not Joseph's father-in-law, concluded proceedings with sentiments which were very much of their time, his idea of the League being that 'they would have better wives, better mothers, and superior members of society'.

Mr Lindley was on the right side of history. He might also have referred to making libraries available for children. The first dedicated children's lending library had opened in Nottingham just two years before. The children of Hebden Bridge would have to wait awhile.

Reading at home

Borrowing of course implies reading at home. Literacy, shorter working hours, railways, and gas and more sophisticated oil or kerosene lamps allowing for reading on dark evenings would all have contributed to making reading a much more widely accessed and enjoyed occupation.

The Hebden Bridge Gas Company at Crow Nest dated back to 1852. (The Crossleys had built their own gas works to supply their mills as early as 1838.) Gas had an extraordinary impact on both street and domestic life. But it did have its downsides. Not only was there the occasional explosion, but 'impure gas gave off a bad smell, blackened walls and ceilings and took gilding off picture frames. It caused headaches, made rooms unbearably hot, and killed off all but the hardiest of household plants. The Victorians loved aspidistras because they were one of the few plants that could survive.'[6]

A fear of contagion

The Spencers with their strong Wesleyan connections would have believed in 'improving' reading for themselves and their family. How far 'improvement' stretched beyond the spiritual we can't say. Any books the family owned were sold off long ago.

They would, though, have been aware in their later years in Hebden Bridge of the arguments for and against a 'free library', that is, a library as we understand it today, without ties to chapel, church or co-op. This was backed by the council in 1902, but funding and premises couldn't be agreed. One argument against was that there was a fear of contagion 'from well-thumbed fiction books'. This is as quoted in the *Hebden Bridge Times* of 15th June 1909, two years after Joseph had closed his business in the town. 'Books are cheap and there is not the same enthusiasm for Free Libraries that there used to be' – curiously similar to arguments we hear in our own time.

19

The Wider World

The Mechanics' Institute

'Nearly every chapel had a mutual improvement society attached.'[1] But some of the old radicalism had seeped away, and chapel members were increasingly respectable and middle class. This was the world in which Joseph and his wife, and their wider family (including the Fieldings and Kershaws) and friends, felt at home.

There had been an early attempt, according to a letter in the *Leeds Mercury* of 8th December 1838, to launch a Mechanics' Institute in Hebden Bridge. It quickly had a library and a reading room, 'between 70 and 80 members', and aspired to four classes, 'mathematical, mechanical, architectural and chemical'. They 'engaged a portion of the Wesleyan Association Chapel in Hebden Bridge as their premises'. It was linked to the successful Leeds Institute, which E. P. Thompson notes was 'from the outset controlled by sponsors from the middle class, and notably by Nonconformist manufacturers'.[2]

Sixteen years later it had not survived. In 1854 Joseph Greenwood was one of three young men 'who canvassed the neighbourhood in the hopes of being enabled to establish a society for mutual improvement'.[3] He was a key figure in the first years of what later became the Hebden Bridge Mechanics' Institute, though he severed his links at an early stage: he and his wife shared their home with the Institute, and relationships became difficult.

The Institute flourished, even without Joseph, but became it seems rather more respectable, with the MP for Halifax in attendance at the annual 'soiree' in 1877, held in the newly completed Co-operative Hall. Glees featured again, as they had at the Hall's opening ceremony. 'A quartet of vocalists, the Huddersfield Orpheus Glee Party, were in attendance to intersperse the speeches etc with glees, songs etc.'

The report delivered to Institute members by the secretary, Mr George Atack, was anything but gleeful. 'The committee desire to say that, in consequence of the Educational Committee of the Co-operative Society commencing an elementary night school, and also science classes, and offering inducements which the committee of the institution were not in a position to offer, the majority of the students who attended the classes at the institution have joined the classes belonging to the Co-operative Society, therefore, after carefully considering the question, the committee came to the conclusion that it would not be advisable to commence any classes during the current session.' (*Todmorden and Hebden Bridge Weekly Advertiser*, 26th October 1877)

The Mechanics' Institute did regroup, and Andrew Bibby notes a lecture given in 1885 by Samuel Fielding in the subject of 'salmon disease and potato blight'.[4]

Another great Hebden Bridge institution, the Literary and Scientific Society, came later. It was founded in 1905, two years before the Spencer family took their final leave of the town.

Oxford comes to Hebden Bridge

If local people in Hebden Bridge couldn't go to Oxford to study, then Oxford could come to Hebden Bridge.

Joseph Greenwood and his colleagues at the Fustian Society took the concept of self-improvement to another level when they established links with Oxford University and inaugurated a series of lectures, the first of which took place in autumn and winter 1886/87.

They were staged in the Co-operative Hall. English history and social and economic history were the subjects. Further lectures a year later were described by Oxford don, G. W. Hudson Shaw, as 'probably by far the most successful course of lectures we have yet had in this most interesting little place'. Crossley Greenwood, Joseph Greenwood's son and Virgil's brother, was one of five students who were awarded distinction in the course examination.

Hudson Shaw gave a further eight lectures over the winter 1888/89, with audiences averaging more than 600 over the period. Lecture subjects included the Age of Elizabeth and (to smaller audiences) Victorian literature.[5]

Lectures were also given in nearby Todmorden. The librarian had concluded his report to the Industrial Co-operative Society (see page 89) by regretting that 'the lectures given last winter were all sparsely attended, with the exception of those given by Rev. S. Kent and J. J. Holyoake, but we venture to hope the lectures for the coming winter season, to be delivered by the Rev. W. Hudson-Shaw, MA, [G. W. Hudson Shaw] will be largely attended, and productive of much good.' Hudson Shaw had switched location from Hebden Bridge to Todmorden. I assume J. J. Holyoake is G. J. Holyoake, a legendary advocate of co-operation, who would have been seventy-three that year. The following year Holyoake was an honoured guest at the coming-of age celebration of the Nutclough Co-operative.

Wesleyans had stood aloof

It is hard to imagine that the Spencers, both Joseph and Emily, would not have been among the larger audiences recorded for the lectures. They despatched Thomas off to a boarding school with serious academic pretensions in 1891. But there is no evidence that Joseph had wider interests beyond work and chapel. In this sense he was very much a Wesleyan. After 1820 'the attitude of official Methodism to the world outside was exclusively evangelistic ...' Rupert Davies refers to a 'conscientious abstention from politics'.[6]

Asa Briggs makes a similar point, in the context of the Anti-Corn Law League. 'Although Wesleyan Methodists stood aloof, Congregationalists, Baptists and Unitarians were often enthusiastic leaguers ...' When politics were at the fiercest, Wesleyans had stood aloof. [7]

E. P. Thompson, despite Methodist missionary parents, could be splendidly vituperative: 'From the outset the Wesleyans fell ambiguously between Dissent and Establishment, and did their utmost to make the worst of both worlds.'[8] Their contribution to the working-class movement came in spite of and not because of the Wesleyan Conference. At the same time he recognised the argument that they were 'indirectly responsible for the growth in the self-confidence and capacity for organisation of working people', not least in their ability to build strong societies at a local level.[9]

It is possible that the new middle-class 'villa Toryism' associated with Lord Salisbury might have had some appeal for Joseph as a merchant and businessman. He moved the family into a smart new house in a prestige location in 1897. That said, there's

Hebden Bridge Liberal Club, 1897, and recently completed, a short walk for Joseph from his new home on Birchcliffe Road, a possible diversion from the demands of shop and chapel. (PHDA-MOS00140)

every reason to believe that Joseph was, in his politics, a mainstream Gladstonian Liberal, and a strong believer in free trade, low tax and self-help.

Education would also have been a big issue. Arguments would have focused around the school boards established by the 1870 Education Act, popular with Nonconformists, and the role of Church schools. They were, at the time the family left Hebden Bridge in 1901, about to come to a head with the 1902 Act, pushed through by a Conservative government, with soon-to-be Prime Minister A. J. Balfour taking the lead.

Joseph would also have seen over five years the emergence, stone by carved stone, of the splendid new Liberal Club building, just below what was to be his new house on Birchcliffe Road. He would almost certainly have been a member, not least for the business connections it would help foster.

The Boer War

One other issue dominated conversation at the time, and that was the Boer War, in which almost half a million British troops, drawn from all over the Empire, fought. It divided the nation, but Lord Salisbury nonetheless won a resounding victory for the Conservatives in the 1900 'khaki' election.

The war was a personal as well as a political issue. A tablet at the entrance to the Hebden Bridge Council Buildings (now the Town Hall) remembers the local soldiers and ambulance volunteers 'who fell in the South African War 1899-1902', and also the reservists 'who readily responded to their country's call', and volunteers from the St John's Ambulance Brigade.

The war also highlighted how unfit the average Englishman was: how would he fare in more protracted warfare, against, for example, a German enemy? The drive for free school meals was not entirely altruistic. It's easy to imagine how these issues might have been debated in the town, not least in the Liberal Club. And at home as well: Thomas would have been twenty-one when the war began in 1899.

Manchester Guardian

How far the *Manchester Guardian* penetrated into Yorkshire I can't say. But as a radical paper it would have had its readership. 'In 1900 two special newspaper trains left Manchester for the North, one running to Wigan ... and the other to Leeds with connections to Bradford and Halifax. By 1900 the *Guardian* reached the principal Yorkshire towns by 4.15 a.m.'

It would surely have been required reading for members of the town's Liberal Club. A meeting of the club in February 1901 at which Joseph's brother-in-law, Dr Walton, was present, had condemned the government's conduct of the war.

As the *Guardian's* historian, David Ayerst, records, 'Public opinion, inflamed by the Jingo press (and that was nearly the whole press) and infuriated by Boer resistance and British defeats, turned its hatred on the M.G. [*Manchester Guardian*] and all those who thought with it.'[10] The *Yorkshire Post* as an avowedly Conservative paper would have aligned with the Jingo press. Events had left the *Guardian* 'the only great morning newspaper which continued to oppose the aims of the government'.

Family gatherings

The two Josephs, Spencer and Greenwood, had a family connection, and this may, or may not, have given them opportunities to discuss events in the wider world. Joseph Greenwood would have had much to say. He had watched strikers as they wound their way through Hebden Bridge at the time of the Plug Riots in 1840.[11] He was a Baptist, not a Wesleyan, and they lacked the top-down restraining hand which inhibited the Wesleyans. He was an activist, setting up the Mechanics' Institute in 1854 and the Nutclough Co-operative in 1870, and a radical, though not a trade union man or socialist. But both Josephs were driven by the need to find new markets and new customers for their businesses, and that would have given them common ground.

20

Moving House

Joseph grew up in one of the old terraced houses on High Street to the west of the town. As the mills extended their operations, and the town expanded, wide areas of valley floor and hillside were taken over. Joseph's first shop after setting up on his own was part of the extensive development of Market Street after 1871. The shop he opened in 1889 was located on land sold for development in 1880, an area known as Black Pit Holme, 'swampy land where the Hebden meets the Calder'.[1]

Brunswick Terrace where the family moved in the mid-1880s ran along the northern side of the modern Brunswick Street and was linked to the Market Street development. The street was built up against the hillside, as a row of 'top and bottom' houses, with, as we've seen, four floors to the front and two at the back.

Heath House

At Heath House, in Mytholm, where the family moved from Brunswick Terrace in 1890, they were away from the building frenzy down in the town. In 1894 Joseph submitted plans for what would be their final move in the town, for a house on the Birchcliffe Estate, on the far side of the valley.[2] With

Heath House, Mytholm, home to the Spencer family from 1890 until 1897. (PHDA-ALC00393)

a family of six children, the eldest sixteen and the youngest a babe in arms, they needed more space. They were also some distance from the centre of town. The schools for the younger children would be Stubbings, built on what had been the Stubbings Estate, some distance away on the lower part of the Birchcliffe hillside, or Central, so called not because it was in the centre of town, which indeed it was, but because schools of this kind had a central hall surrounded by classrooms.

They would be leaving behind, probably with some regret, a handsome brick double-fronted villa, with a central bay, well above the valley, and facing south-east. They occupied one half, and maybe at some point the whole building. A field, accessed by steps which ran down from the front door, opened out below. A terrace at the foot of the hill and a row of three-storey tenement-style houses just behind were the only houses nearby. In short, they had space, clean air, views and greenery. It was an unusual house for its time, and for the town.

In the move's favour would have been the superior space and facilities of a new home, especially one which they could specify themselves. Joseph would have had memories of growing up on High Street, with limited space, and the family working at home, and an ashpit and toilets in a shared court out the back. And as a successful shopkeeper he would now own a house that matched his new status.

Status

With expectations went status. The working class were not of course a homogeneous group. The upper working class, which would include artisans, clerks, tradesmen and shopkeepers, aspired to better houses, and a better quality of life. Joseph and his family living at Heath House may have fitted that upper-working-class profile but as a successful shopkeeper and good Wesleyan he would have seen himself as aspiring middle class.

On Birchcliffe Road he and Emily took that new status very seriously. Joseph would have taken responsibility for the design, plans and building of the house. 'Building had become an economic activity where success depended on everything being minutely predetermined.'[3] That we assume would have been Joseph's responsibility. Emily's focus would have been all matters domestic: 'the running of the house was considered an immensely serious matter.'[4] Her role was as mistress of the house. Outside the home she exercised her practical skills in ladies' sewing classes and the like. There's no evidence of any paid employment.

There had always been 'a refusal of the better classes to live in close proximity to the lower classes. A change of class meant moving house, moving into another district.'[5] Hebden Bridge was too small for significant separation, and indeed this was turned on its head when locals gave the name of 'snob row' to the new Birchcliffe Road development. Posh developments would normally be shielded and out of site. 'Snob row', climbing the hill above St George's Square, could hardly have been more visible.

Class mobility markedly increased in the nineteenth century. The new middle class, which had its own gradations, looked to protect its space. 'The rules of good society became stricter so they did not get blurred with the increased mobility between classes … some of the agreements for middling houses in the middle of the century contain more stipulations than those for the best houses, to make doubly sure that standards were kept, the standards at each level of the hierarchy.'[6]

Joseph must have been confident that he, and his family, and his business, could live up to the requirements of his new status. He was heavily mortgaged and he was taking a risk, but the economy locally and nationally was expanding fast and he had ambitions. He had branches in several Lancashire towns as well as Hebden Bridge. Had he stayed the course he might have been another Hepworths[7] or Fifty Shilling Tailors, the company founded by Harry Price in Leeds in 1903, which grew to have 399 stores, and was renamed John Collier when it was taken over in the 1950s.

Trade as a tailor would once upon a time have fixed you forever in the social hierarchy. But no more: 'on the whole, divisions by pay replaced earlier patterns of division by trade.'[8]

Birchcliffe Road

In 1895 the *Todmorden Advertiser and Hebden Bridge Newsletter* had a short piece which ran as follows: 'The amended plan submitted by Mr Joseph Spencer for the reception to a dwelling-house in Birchcliffe Road was recommended to be passed.' It had earlier been 'put back on account of the drains as shown not being satisfactory'. There could be sanitation problems high on the hillside as much as down in the town. The Nuisance and Building Committee that handled such matters was vigilant.

The land on the Birchcliffe Estate had been sold off for individual houses on a house-by-house basis, moving up the hill. The first plans had been submitted by John Redman, a wholesale clothier, in 1887. Joseph and family were the last to contract and the last to move in. The houses are broadly similar in terms of stone, windows, roofs and the like. But the new owners had considerable room for manoeuvre, as the variations in height and gables demonstrate. Separate plans had to be submitted to the council for each house. And plans could be turned down, with consequent delays.

Ordnance Survey map from 1905 showing Birchcliffe Road (left centre), the new Baptist chapel (right) and (to the north) Nutclough Mill. Reproduced with the permission of the National Library of Scotland)

The 1897 electoral register has the Spencer's address down as Brentwood, Birchcliffe Road, so it must have been that year they moved to their new home. There is also a mention of a plot of land on the Birchcliffe Estate in an indenture of 1899: 'A further charge on shop, hereditaments and premises in Market Street …' Joseph may have been borrowing to fund a final payment on the completion of the house.

'Snob row'

Stone as we would expect in a Pennine town dominated in local building. There would be no need for brick for structural work behind a stone façade, as happened elsewhere. Mechanised quarries with steam-powered saws would have ensured the ready availability of stone for the rapid growth in house building in the town, and indeed across the Upper Calder Valley. Brentwood was typical also in using stone with a rough 'rubble' finish as opposed the smooth ashlar finish often used on public buildings.

There were a number of stone quarries in the immediate vicinity of the town. The 1881 census lists 126 men as quarrymen. There was also an abundance of skilled stonemasons, glaziers, joiners, plumbers, slaters and plasterers. As a 2021 exhibition, 'Who Built Hebden Bridge', at Hebden Bridge Town Hall highlighted, the town could draw on an abundance of specialist craftsmen.

Nikolaus Pevsner in his original West Riding volume in the *Buildings of England* series mentions only the parish church in Hebden Bridge. Mills (he's referring in this case to Halifax) may be 'visually exciting and inspire awe, but with architectural beauty they have nothing to do'. As for the domestic houses ('villas') of the period, they were not part of the remit he gave himself. But he might have looked kindly on Birchcliffe Road, where the houses were built with an impressive eye for detail.[9]

The plan and specification would have been the work of a local architect, who is likely to have been John Sutcliffe, whose obituary recalled 'a designer of a host of buildings dotted about the district, including many public premises and better-class houses. Quiet and unassuming in disposition, he was a typical gentleman of the professional classes.'

The building has changed over the years but is today in most respects as it was in the 1890s. The double gable is a distinctive feature. The gable wall to the left has a dressed stone porch flush with the wall, hall behind, narrow columns either side, and arch above. To the right a four-light two-storey bay extends out below the gable.

The original plans from 1894 refer to a drawing room and dining room opening off a hall with a woodblock floor, off which also open a breakfast room and, at the back of the house, a kitchen, with its own cooking range. There are four bedrooms on the first floor, and two more on the second. Stairs lead down from the hall to a 'wash kitchen' with its own cooking range and basin, and a pantry behind. The house would have been gas-lit at least at basement and ground-floor level. The accommodation would have allowed for a maid, but the 1901 census records refers only to family.

From a distance the 'snob row' houses give an impression of unity, such as we find in Georgian terraces, and the smart brick and often multi-storey terraces of Victorian cities, and indeed the endless terraces of working-class housing. Closer to, seen from the street, the sameness is superficial, and the architectural detail well repays close inspection[10]

How others saw the house is well demonstrated by its description in the sale document when the house was put up for auction in 1902. 'Recently erected at great expense' it was 'situate in a very convenient position for a gentleman in or out of business'.

The front elevation from the architect's plans for Brentwood have survived to this day, but in a very fragile condition.

There's every reason to suppose that Emily had her own copy of *Mrs Beeton's Book of Household Management*, first published back in 1861. She would have taken on board the requirements of household management. An interesting survival from the Spencer family home at Brentwood is the cooking range, down in the basement. It isn't, however, the 'Crabtree's Patent Close Fire Range' recommended in the 1891 edition of Mrs Beeton, but the suitably patriotic 'Yorkshire' range, as described by Peter Brears in his splendid book, *Traditional Food in the South Pennines*.

With 'a coal-burning grate flanked by a perpetual oven on one side and a hob or side boiler on the other', Yorkshire ranges had become 'a standard fitting in numerous terraces erected for mill workers'. And also for the Spencers, though theirs was, as we've seen, literally below stairs.

Coal was a game changer, for the mills and at home. It was abundant and cheap, and the West Riding collieries were not far away. Another great change was to diet. The days of oats were numbered. They were the only crop that would grow at elevated altitudes and in cold and wet conditions. For the Spencers as for everyone in the town oatcakes and porridge would have been the everyday foods.

As Brears points out, as the population grew the demand for oats exceeded supply. Supplies were imported from outside the area – but so too was wheat. 'The larger thinner yeast-raised oatcakes had already replaced the thick crisp oatcake which required only a bakestone, frying pan or oven.' But they in turn, from the 1880s, were superseded by bread made from white bread flour, bought from local grocers (no doubt, for many in Hebden Bridge, from the Co-op) where flour 'was scooped out of tubs into the customer's own "flour poke", a stout cotton or linen bag resembling a pillow slip'. (Porridge, it's worth pointing out, never lost its popularity.)

These were more than just changes to diet, they were lifestyle changes, and it may be that for the Spencers their move to Heath House marked the turning-point. The middle-class world of Mrs Beeton became readily available. And that also included meat. For mill workers 'bits of bacon and offal' had been as close as they came to meat. For hill farmers it had been different. But as the Calder Valley opened up to the world in the late nineteenth century, and prices tumbled, beef, pork and mutton became part of everyday life.

Neighbours

Neighbours included the Pickles family at Briggville, just two doors away. George was a successful engineer and businessman. The families would have known each other well through their involvement with Salem Chapel. Lilian and Lillie Pickles were of a similar age and probably friends. They were the only girls in their shorthand class, or indeed any of the shorthand classes, in the town.

An even closer Salem connection lay four doors away, where lived a Wesleyan minister, William Lake. This would have been a smart residence for an itinerant minister.

A further Salem connection lay at nearby Clareville. Angelina Greenwood is listed as head of household in the 1901 census. With Angelina lived her sister, Clara, and her husband, Tom Smith, Joseph's friend, and the choirmaster at the chapel.

Another near neighbour, and quite probably friend, was John Shaw, who lived at Glen Royd, a few doors away down the hill. It was Shaw who took over responsibility for Brentwood after the family vacated the house and before its sale in August 1902.

21

From Township to Town

The population of the wider area, taking in Wadsworth, Heptonstall and Erringden, grew on one estimate from 10,672 in 1851 to 13,083 in 1901, and on another from 10,800 in 1861 to 15,700 in 1891. The latter figures are taken from *A Short History of Todmorden*. The author refers to Hebden Bridge as 'one of the chief centres in England for the manufacture of fustian and ready-made clothing'. He is impressed by its prosperity: 'Today [the book was published in 1912] the hillsides are lined with rows of cottages and dotted with new houses that indicate the prosperity of the district.'[1]

People had deserted the hills and moved to the town as the big mills and mechanised weaving took over from the handloom, bringing to an end the old 'dual economy' whereby a household could readily support itself on the two activities of farming and making cloth.

But they also came in from far afield, as Manchester and the Lancashire cotton towns had experienced with the influx of the Irish earlier in the century.

It does seem that the Irish were none too welcome in Hebden Bridge. An incident from August 1839 during the building of the Manchester and Leeds Railway when a group of Englishmen 'united to drive all the Irish from the line' suggests an early hostility.[2] Census returns from more than sixty years later for Dawson City, which housed the labourers building the Walshaw Green reservoirs, demolished 'the myth that all Navvies were Irish labourers'.[3] There was much more of a welcome for immigrant Irish among the large community of their compatriots in nearby Halifax.

Unusually among textile towns, in part no doubt because of the constraints imposed by space but also because, as a town, it was a late arrival compared to its neighbours, Hebden Bridge held on to its distinctive 'local' identity.

Hebden Bridge Local Board

As the town had grown the old townships had seemed less and less appropriate. On one side of Hebden Water lay Wadsworth, on the other Heptonstall. Further to the west lay Stansfield, which extended all the way to the border with Todmorden. Across the river Calder lay Erringden. New

Looking east to the Birchcliffe hillside, 1880, Foster Mill to the left, Nutclough Mill centre. (PHDA-ALC00398)

Looking east to the Birchcliffe hillside: Nutclough Mill centre foreground, new Birchcliffe Road houses climbing the hill, centre right, c.1898. (PHDA-DEF00255)

boundaries were proposed and Joseph and Emily as children would have seen the new Hebden Bridge District Board come into being in 1866 (reconstituted in 1871 as the Local Board). After further boundary changes the Local Board became Hebden Bridge Urban District Council in 1894.

The original gasworks for the town had been established at Crow Nest in 1852. The local council took it over in 1895 and the new gasworks opened on the same site in 1907. The town did not gain its own electricity works until 1904 but electric trams reached Hebden Bridge in 1901, just as the Spencers were leaving the town. The water supply had been a serious concern for the whole region, alleviated when Widdop reservoir opened above the town in 1870. Joseph and Emily would have seen the disruption caused by the building, and the benefits. Sanitation as we've seen was arguably the biggest issue of all, and the hardest to resolve.

One success story was street lighting, but it hadn't all gone smoothly. The Lighting and Paving Committee had in the 1860s attempted, as a voluntary body, to maintain street lighting and improve the roads by subscription. They put their case for a properly constituted public body to an inquiry in 1866. 'During the past winter the subscription had been so inadequate the Committee had been forced to leave the town in darkness for a month.' One of the first decisions of the new Board was to order the gas lamps in the town 'to be lighted at dusk and put out at 11 p.m., 12 on Saturdays'.[4] I quoted earlier Emily's father Thomas Walton's grumble to the Board about the lighting at Foster Mill. This was 1872: change is only smooth in retrospect.

Traffic jams

Paving in the form of setts was a priority as the town expanded. Walking up the steep valleys would have been the norm, though some of the big houses did have stables, and distinctive mounting blocks in the street.

For carriers and hauliers it was a very different story. An article from the *Halifax Courier* of 25th May 1889 reported on a meeting to discuss a new bridge, which became St George's Bridge, across Hebden Water. Businesses in the Hanging Royd area and traffic along Old Gate were much in need of the relief a new bridge would provide. Detailed information was laid before the meeting to demonstrate just how crowded Old Gate could be.

There were in the area '23 manufactories and workshops ... 24 out warehouses and stables ... 182 residences ... also 22 houses in course of erection.'

Traffic was as follows: '17th May – 262 horses with carts, etc, and 15 heavy loads, and 12 times during the day was the road blocked. 18th May – 237 horses, etc, 19 heavy loads, and 18 blocks.'

The case for a new bridge was well made, but it also gives an idea of how horse-drawn traffic could crowd a growing town. The quiet stretches of empty setts that survive to this day would have looked very different back then.

The opening ceremony for the bridge (funded by public subscription topped up by a West Riding County Council grant) took place in November 1893, with the crowd on the bridge improvising their own ceremony, while the town's dignitaries marked the occasion with a smart dinner at which, as the *Hebden Bridge Times* noted, the speeches were 'many and long'.

Windows stashed with all kinds of goods

East of Market Street and at the heart of the modern town, lies an area, located between Commercial Street, New Road and Bridge Gate, known as the Croft. Until the 1860s it was an open field.*

Habergrams, a popular Market Street shop, advertising its wide stock of Christmas goods. (PHDA-ALC00337)

Over the period 1870–1900 the area was transformed. Impressive buildings such as the Hope Chapel, the Co-op Hall and the Hope Chapel's Sunday School extension, which later became the library, were built during this period. There were problems of water supply and drainage to overcome as there would have been with the Market Street developments.

New shops were opening, stashed with all kinds of goods, also new public houses. The police station opened there, and banks asserted their status by building impressive new buildings for themselves, the first being the Hebden

---

* Much of this section draws on a report of a talk given by Michael Peel to the Hebden Bridge Local History Society.[5]

Bridge Joint Stock Company, on the corner of Albert and Hope Street, which opened its doors in 1874. And, just as the Spencer family were leaving town, in 1901, the tram arrived.

Hebden Bridge, tram arrival, 1905. (PHDA-DAH00215)

It was also an area of industrial development, with a gas holder, timber yard, iron foundry and textile mills, and an iron and tinplate works producing tin trunks. When the family moved to Birchcliffe Road they would have looked directly down on this area of extraordinary activity. It's hard not to believe that when the family moved away to quieter territories in Cheshire the children at least didn't miss it. Suburbia would have been an arid place by comparison.

The other major bank to open in the town at this time was the Manchester and Liverpool District Bank, on the corner of Crown Street and New Road. It is more than likely that Joseph with his already strong Manchester connections banked with the District.[6] (See page 57.)

Emily and the children would have been more concerned with the shops. The changes over a short period of time had been remarkable: Joseph had only moved into his newly built Market Street premises in 1889. *Kelly's Directory* for 1901[7] lists all the commercial premises in the town. Cloggers were a reminder of harsh day-to-day realities. A cycle agent looked to the future.

On Market Street itself as well as multiple tailors and outfitters were grocers, butchers, 'fried fish dealers', and boot and shoemakers, also a chemist, a confectioner, a 'fancy dealer and tobacconist', a hairdresser, a furniture dealer, and a glass and china dealer. There were refreshment rooms at number 12 (Lello's) and at number 35 (James Hartley). Joseph's immediate neighbours were a confectioner, stationer, 'musical instrument warehouse' and chemist.

A child stands innocently at the door of William Dehner, Wholesale and Retail Pork Butcher, 22 Bridge Gate, Hebden Bridge. (PHDA-RUD00158)

The cliché, 'a nation of shopkeepers', which is usually traced back to Adam Smith, came true in Victorian times in a very literal sense, and our high (and market) streets bear witness to this day.

There is just one caveat to all this. Many shopkeepers had serious competition from a well-established and very popular player – the local Co-op.

'… a very commanding and bold appearance'

By 1868 there were three branches of the Co-op in the town. By 1875 the existing premises in Bridge Gate were too small and in 1877 new premises, built of stone, of 'a very commanding and bold appearance', opened with a main entrance on Crown Street. The businesses were to be 'grocery, drapery and millinery, furniture, boots and shoes'. 'Clogging' is also mentioned. These were situated on the ground floor, the reading room and storerooms above, and above that the hall, 'a spacious room large enough to accommodate, we should guess, 800 people'. Boilers in the basement provided warmth and 'motive power for the sugar choppers, coffee grinders, etc'. It remained open until 6 p.m. on Saturday.[8]

The number of members at the time of opening was 1,308, and since the formation of the society 'more than £50,000 has been paid in dividends and interest'. 'No wonder some of you will be struck by this amount, but remember this has been paid to members, the working classes of the small village [scaling down what was already a town!], which has gone to elevate and lift them up the social scale.'

Competition may have come for Joseph from the drapery and millinery ranges. But there is no indication that they had any involvement with ready-to-wear or bespoke tailoring.

Solicitors

Also recorded in *Kelly's Directory* were solicitors.[9] They were of course pivotal to all commercial and domestic activity and loomed large in Joseph's life. He would have required good legal advice, not least because of the sizeable mortgages he took out. He was, it seems, slow to pay off his first mortgage, taken out in 1884. This didn't stop him taking out further mortgages, not least to fund the building of his new house on Birchcliffe Road.

His solicitor, the firm run by William Henry Sutcliffe, may also have advised on insurance. Joseph would have been insured against fire, and no doubt against accidents more widely defined. Policies covering railway accidents and steam boiler explosions were an important development. Accident insurance was one more area where, with a tenfold increase in the number of insurers, the market had changed beyond all recognition by the end of the century.

William Henry had along with his brothers, John and James, inherited the long-standing Sutcliffe business (with members of the family listed as articled to the firm as far back as 1756) from their father, another William.[10] William Henry, born in 1854, was the same age as Joseph, but his family were by this time local gentry, and substantial landowners, and they moved in different circles. Joseph's main contact was always with an articled clerk.

22

The Spencer Children

Joseph and Emily, with Lilian and Thomas in the back row, and Norman, Wesley, Robert and Reginald in the front row. A photograph taken in 1895 or 1896.

We can only speculate why Joseph and Emily put off extending their family for almost a decade after Lilian was born. It was a time when Joseph was setting up on his own, and it may simply be that they considered two children more than enough. This could be put down to competent family planning, or there may have been babies who were stillborn other than a single one recorded in 1899.

Norman, the third child, was born nine years after Lilian, in 1889. Three other boys, Wesley, Reginald and Robert, followed. Thomas and Lilian, and their younger brothers, were in effect two separate families, and when it came to education required entirely different approaches.

The younger children, four boys, all born 1889 and later, would almost certainly have been educated in their early years at the board schools in Hebden Bridge. When they finally moved to Cheshire in 1903 they continued their schooling at the local board school there.

Maypole dancing on the Birchcliffe hillside, 1894. (PHDA-ALC00198)

How much freedom they were allowed outside school hours is impossible to know. They may have been corralled into maypole dancing, which required high levels of discipline. The boys in their pace-egg costumes in the photo below look, on the other hand, to be enjoying their freedom. Whether the Spencer children would have been allowed to take part I can't say. The elders of Salem Chapel may well have frowned on such frivolity even though pace-egging was a long-established custom.

Pace-egg players, St George's Square, Hebden Bridge, late nineteenth century.. (PHDA-EIL00114)

Pace-egg plays, with their mock-combat scenes typically involving a hero, who could be St George, and a villain, in the form of the Bold Slasher or the Black Prince, also a comic doctor, who revives the villain, and Toss-pot, playing the fool, have a long history. Whether it mirrors death and resurrection, or winter's passage into spring, seems entirely secondary. Players and their supporters used to be given eggs. 'Pace' is an abbreviation of 'pascha', Easter in Latin. The plays were, and are, performed every Good Friday. The ribbons and streamers and blackened faces were part of the traditional attire. The tradition survives in Hebden Bridge and nearby Midgley and Heptonstall.[1]

There were of course quieter activities. Thomas may have been, to judge from his school prize, a keen young astronomer. Other children would have been, with the hills on the doorstep, keen young naturalists – following a strong local tradition. Still others may have been fascinated by the trains. Thomas's younger brother, Wesley (christened Charles Wesley), had a lifelong love of steam trains. The first 'spotters' guides' didn't appear until a few decades later, but they were catering to a long-established fascination.

Group portraits

The Spencer family in the group portrait which begins this chapter are all smartly attired. Lilian looks to be there under duress. Reginald has a conventional collar and jacket but his kilt, sporran, plaid and Glengarry hat (and there's possibly a small ceremonial knife attached to his sock) put him in a tradition of dressing up boys which dates back to 'the 1840s when Queen Victoria and Prince Albert began dressing the young princes in kilts'.[2]

Joseph looks as if he wouldn't be trifled with. But on other occasions, it seems, such group portraits could get a little out of hand. There's a disarming and slightly chaotic innocence about the photograph overleaf, which looks to belong to a similar period to the Spencer photograph. The group appears to be in imminent danger of collapsing down the slope.

What looks to be a gentle Sunday afternoon walk interrupted by a photo shoot, probably 1890s. (PHDA-ALC06375)

What is remarkable to a modern eye is the range of hats. In the family portrait both Joseph and Emily are wearing straw boaters, maybe Lilian as well. The men in the photograph above are wearing a trilby and a bowler. The boys wear caps. A tall hat is worn with a touch of style in the back row. Everyone, with the exception of one cheerful girl, is, as was the convention, resisting the temptation to smile.

School boards

We looked at education in Hebden Bridge, and how it might have affected Joseph and Emily and their parents, in an earlier section. But what of Thomas, born 1878, and Lilian, born 1880?

It was a time of rapid and radical change. The 1870 Elementary Education Act provided for the election of school boards which would provide for schools paid for out of an education rate. Salem Sunday School had been the location of a crowded meeting in support of Nonconformist candidates for election to the first Todmorden District School Board, established in 1874. Mytholm Church School held a similar meeting backing Church candidates. The result for Todmorden as a whole was seven Chapel candidates elected and two Church.[3]

Mytholm Church School had existing status as a recognised National school. The Academy which existed at Salem Chapel had no official status.[4]

But it had from 1874 the advantage of a brand-new Sunday school. Nonconformists could hardly support education for their children in a Church of England establishment and plans were laid down for a new board school at the other (eastern) end of town. Salem Sunday School provided temporary accommodation until the school was able to move into new buildings, occupied today by Stubbings Infant School, in 1878.

'Staffing and accommodation were based on classes of sixty' and such was the overcrowding that the Senior Department moved to temporary accommodation in 1882, again at the Salem Sunday School, before a new 'Central school' opened in 1884. Extra money for the original school meant smaller class sizes, and new accommodation at the Central school included 'a cookery room, a chemistry laboratory and demonstration room, and five more classrooms'.[5]

As young children Thomas and Lilian would have been educated at the Stubbings or the Central school, though there is a caveat regarding Lilian, which I touch on below. The school at Mytholm was much closer but chapel loyalties would have required a walk across town to the new school.

The question for Joseph and Emily would have been what to do with Thomas and Lilian, born 1878 and 1880, when they were past the age of ten. 'A child between 10 and 13 shall not be required to attend school if such a child has reached Standard Six,' ran a byelaw of April 1893.[6] Assuming both children reached Standard Six by the age of ten or eleven, how might they continue their education beyond that time? For Thomas the answer, at a cost of £30 a year, was to send the boy away, to boarding school.

Thomas at Woodhouse Grove

From 1891 to 1894 he was a pupil at Woodhouse Grove School, in Apperley, near Bradford. Lilian was also, we believe, educated outside the state system.

Woodhouse Grove School had been founded, in 1811, to educate the sons of itinerant (never more than two years in post) Wesleyan ministers.*. 'Their poverty and constant relocation made it difficult to provide a stable education for their sons.' Strict discipline underpinned the teaching. John Wesley had written that 'a wise parent ... should begin to break [a child's] will the moment it appears'.[7]

A 'milder mode' of treating boys may have been followed in practice, but the school's educational aspirations remained limited. The school

---

* The school has a Brontë connection: it was the school's first master, John Fennell, who brought his wife's niece, Maria Branwell, from Cornwall, to help at the school, and introduced her to his friend from earlier Shropshire days, Patrick Brontë. The young couple fell in love and married in December 1812.

committee in 1856 required all new boys to read tolerably, to write simple sentences from dictation and 'to show a satisfactory acquaintance with the four simple rules of Arithmetic and the first part of the Catechism'.[8]

In 1883 the school was refounded, as a Methodist middle-class boarding and day school, admitting boys 'from a wider spectrum of backgrounds'. The school's biographer describes it as 'catering for laymen's sons whose children were not particularly affluent'. Fees were kept low at £30 per annum, one reason why it attracted a new cohort of parents 'who had no genuine intellectual ambitions for their sons but wanted them to receive a boarding school education which was already beginning to have an aura of ultra-respectability'.[9] This is a very blunt appraisal. Joseph may have had genuine intellectual aspirations for Thomas. But the reference to respectability, to status, may not be too wide of the mark.

Sending Thomas away to school would certainly have set him apart from the majority of boys in Hebden Bridge. The headmaster, Arthur Vintner, was keen for the refounded school to have many of the aspirations of a public school. By 1885 pupils were playing regular cricket matches against other schools. Rugby and fives also featured, and lacrosse, for which the school became well known, was introduced in 1889. The school swimming bath opened in 1892.[10] All a far cry from Hebden Bridge.

The school cycling club, 1895. (Cycling club photograph reproduced by permission of Woodhouse Grove School)

There's no indication that Thomas had any particular sporting ability. But he was proficient academically, and won the form prize for the Second Year in July 1892. The prize was *Sun, Moon and Stars: A Book for Beginners*. Thomas was following in the tradition of a pupil of the school, from an earlier period, one Joseph Slugg, a keen astronomer, who became 'one of the most successful populariser of science of his day'.[11]

Thomas would, at home in Hebden Bridge, have been helped by the absence of air pollution. This was a big issue in industrial towns, but an elevated location and prevailing westerly winds would have guaranteed Hebden Bridge skies clearer and so much better for stargazing than the bigger towns downriver.

Woodhouse Grove form prize to Thomas Spencer, 1892.

Thomas's choice of prize suggests an early interest in science: he would have been fourteen years old. Over thirty years before there had been a much-heralded debate in Oxford between Thomas (T. H.) Huxley and Bishop Wilberforce. Darwin's *On the Origin of Species* had been published the previous year. 'In the debate, [Wilberforce] threw the full force of his theological training into upholding the idea of biblical creation, refuting Darwin's picture of evolution through natural selection.' Huxley asserted that he would 'rather have a miserable ape for a grandfather' than a man of great ability and influence who 'introduced ridicule into a grave scientific discussion'.[12]

Where did the Wesleyans stand in this argument? Back in 1854 a compilation of articles from *The Methodist Magazine* had been published under the title of 'The Youth's Instructor and Guardian', with schoolteachers its primary target. The very first article (out of almost 600 pages) had focused on Archbishop Usher's famous chronology which established on seemingly sound biblical evidence the year of creation as having been 4004 BC.[13]

'Usher's name is now most familiarly associated with his great work on chronology. Those "Annals" have been widely used as a chronological standard, and it is well known that the years noted in the margins of our English Bibles are determined from their authority.'

Thomas's school prize, published in 1891, attempted to accommodate both sides of the argument. A preface by a professor of astronomy at Oxford argued in the book's preface that 'in the Book of Nature, side by side with the Book of Revelation, we may learn some things about our Father in Heaven'. The book's author, Agnes Giberne, focused admirably on the current state of scientific knowledge, but nonetheless reminded her young readers that 'Whether suns and world full-grown, created as in an instant – whether vast masses of flaming gas, to be gradually cooled and "framed" into shape – whichever may have come first, and whichever may have been the order of God's working, still that "first" was made by Him; still He throughout was the Master-builder.'[14]

Lilian – home or away?

For middle-class boys of newly affluent parents beyond board-school age there were smart boarding schools. There were no direct equivalents for girls. Lilian's mother at a young age had been a cotton winder. Putting Lilian to work aged thirteen in one of the local mills would have been out of the question. Options for her would include teaching, clerical work – or, in her case, working in her father's shop. But not yet.

She claimed in conversation with her grandchildren that she had only had two years of schooling. It may be that Emily, in the 1880s, with just the two children, thought she could give Lilian a better education at home. It may also be that Lilian is referring to two years she spent away from home *after* she finished her board-school education, when she would have been ten or eleven years old.

She mentioned that she had spent time at a school called Oaklands, in the

Grange-over-Sands area. It was described in 1882/3 as a 'ladies boarding and day school', but there is no other record of the school. There were as many as ten such schools in the area in the 1880s and 1890s, and for some there was a Wesleyan connection. 'Most of the schools were established in converted large houses and they generally adopted the name of the house as the school name.' The prospectus for one of the schools, Sunnybrae School for Girls, albeit from a later date, indicates that the school had serious aspirations for its pupils:

'The aim of the school, in addition to the ordinary educational work, is to develop in a pleasant home atmosphere the intellectual and physical faculties of the pupils, with a careful training of character to prepare them for the work of life.'[15]

We do know that in the 1891 census Lilian is recorded as living away at the home of a Wesleyan minister based at Girsby Grange near Darlington, who we assume is a family friend. She is described as a scholar.

Sending Lilian away, as they had done with her brother, would also allow Emily to focus her attentions on what was effectively a second family, with four boys born between 1889 and 1894. Later in the decade Lilian would have been enlisted to help with the boys. It would give her the experience she needed for her role as a governess a few years later.

She may also have helped in the Hebden Bridge shop. She is recorded as taking local classes in business-related subjects. She passed Elementary Shorthand in a class in which she was one of only two girls, the other being her neighbour, Lillie Pickles. In Advanced Shorthand she was on her own – the only girl.[16]

A sense of how Lilian was as a child may be gleaned from Lilian's granddaughter Barbara's memories of her granny in old age. Her days 'would begin with *The Times* crossword, the full one with quotations, some of which had to be looked up. She had a grand piano which she would play with accomplishment, music like Chopin although her listening was not particularly highbrow, being Liberace and Mantovani, popular classical players. She read very heavy [weighty both to hold and in content] history books.'

A family business?

With the education of his two eldest children complete, just what were Joseph's ambitions at this stage for his business? In 1899 the family was living in a very smart house, Thomas had completed what was for his time and community an expensive education, and Joseph celebrated his son's coming of age with a trip for staff and friends, sixty people in all, to Southport.

Thomas Spencer, c.1899, maybe taken to mark his 21st birthday.

I mentioned J. Hepworth & Son earlier. Joseph Hepworth had set up his business as 'juvenile clothing manufacturers' in Leeds in 1864. In 1878 his son Norris Rhodes Hepworth had become a partner. On Norris's initiative they cut out the middleman and set up as retailers. By 1891 they had ninety-one branches, and in time became 'the largest clothing and manufacturer and retailer in the country'.[17] (The business survives to this day, albeit by a circuitous route, as Next.)

It is possible that Joseph Spencer had Norris in mind when he brought his son, Thomas, into the business. He had shops in several Lancashire towns and the logic would have been to expand further. With many enterprises it's the son who builds on a father's foundations, and takes the business to new markets, and to a different level. It could be, by a reverse logic, that Joseph had in mind for Thomas to develop the manufacturing side of the business. Again, cutting out the middleman. Or simply to open new outlets.

But Thomas was not a natural entrepreneur. His education was more academic and not, literally, on the shop floor. The shop floor would have been a better training. As we will see Thomas managed the shop in Hebden Bridge for his father after the family left town. But there's a sense that his heart was never in it.

23

An Abrupt Departure

Sold at auction

Moving into the house of Birchcliffe Road in 1897 must have been the fulfilment of a dream. It remains to this day an impressive-looking house, and retains the name Brentwood on the gatepost given to it by Joseph and Emily.*

That business was also flourishing a report in the *Todmorden & District News* of 30th June 1899 would seem to confirm:

> COMING OF AGE.—On Wednesday, Mr. Thomas Spencer, son of Mr. Joseph Spencer, merchant tailor, attained the age of 21, and for the purpose of celebrating the event the whole of Mr. Spencer's employes and several friends, making up a party of about 60, took part in a picnic to Southport. They journeyed in two saloons attached to the 7-16 a.m. train, arriving at their destination about a quarter past ten. The day was spent in an enjoyable fashion. A capital dinner was partaken of at Hey's dining rooms. Home was reached about half-past eleven. The hero the day has been the recipient of a number of presents, including a handsome writing desk from the employes.

Two saloons specially attached to the train carried the party. This is a very public display of confidence in family and the future. And yet, just two years later, in 1901, the family left the town, abruptly it would seem, and the following year the house was sold at auction.

Joseph and Thomas continued running the business on Market Street, but Emily, Lilian and the four young boys moved away. The family had, as we shall see, good reason for staying out of sight of friends and neighbours. It is probable they planned to return to Hebden Bridge later in the year, but events dictated otherwise.

Two documents, a letter and a mortgage, dated 1st January 1902, mark a

---

* Brentwood. Why choose the name of a town in Essex? There may be a Blackpool connection. 'Brentwood', a house on Blackpool's South Shore, had been the home of a retired Wesleyan minister, George Dickenson, based at one time in Hebden Bridge. Blackpool may well have been a popular holiday destination for the Spencers, though it was to Southport that Joseph took his staff to celebrate Thomas's 21st birthday.

point of no return. They refer to a transfer of Joseph's several mortgages, and the assurance policies associated with them, from Joseph to a local solicitor, John Shaw, a near-neighbour on Birchcliffe Road.[1] Also mentioned is 'the principal sum of two thousand four hundred pounds now owing …'

Instead of re-mortgaging he handed all rights in his properties ('All and Singular the hereditaments described in the First and Third Schedules', which covered both the shop and the house) to John Shaw. Shaw in return advanced a further sum of £1,000 to Joseph, repayable at the beginning of July, after which time Shaw would have 'the statutory power of sale'.

The *Todmorden Advertiser and Hebden Bridge Newsletter* reported on the sale of the house, by auction, in August, the receipts from which would have paid off part of the mortgage. It would seem that at this point Joseph took out a new mortgage on the shop, with William Sutcliffe and John Shaw the joint mortgagees. They appear again in the story when Joseph sells the shop five years later.

There were as we will see good reasons for the family's precipitate departure, and the subsequent sale of the house. Joseph had a successful business, and he'd proved adept in juggling mortgages over the previous sixteen years. But regular mortgage repayments require regular cashflow, and that in turn requires total focus. Joseph needed to be focused and the events of 1901 must have been a mighty distraction.

'The excllent dwelling-house called Brentwood'

'Last night at the White Horse Hotel, Mr Dan Crossley offered for public competition the excellent dwelling-house called Brentwood, owned and occupied by Mr Jos. Spencer, and situate in Birchcliffe road. The property is freehold …' The house is described in grandiloquent terms: '… recently erected at great expense, and situate in a very convenient position for a gentleman in or out of business'.[2]

The purchaser was Vivian Sutcliffe. There is a plaque marking his ownership on the wall of the house. His father, Thomas, had 'built and expanded the Regent Works factory at Hangingroyd which at the time of his death in 1901 provided work for about 220 people. Under his only son, Vivian, the business continued to prosper and during WW1 was mainly engaged in making khaki trousers for the Army.'[3] It was one of the companies recorded by Tom Greenwood[4] as combining in 1901 with the largest dyeing firm (Moss Bros Ltd) in the district to form the English Fustian Manufacturing Co. Ltd.

Joseph and family would have enjoyed their status among the high-fliers of Hebden Bridge. But father and son, staying behind and running the business in the town, now no longer had a home. Where might they have stayed? The family of Eli Fielding, Joseph's brother-in-law by his elder sister, is one possibility. The Greenwoods, neighbours on Birchcliffe Road, are another. They may even have camped out above the shop.

The glory days it seemed were over. Quite why events had worked out as they did would have been a puzzle to friends and associates, to their Wesleyan colleagues, and indeed to their customers. But the Spencers had a secret, to be kept it seems at all costs.

24
Family Scandal

The moment Emily came across a letter, dated 23rd March, to her daughter from the Salvation Army in Halifax everything changed. Lilian had made contact with the Army on her own initiative. It would seem she had missed her period and feared the worst. She gave birth to a boy, Geoffrey, in a Salvation Army hostel on Mare Street in Hackney on 20th September 1901. The father was a local Hebden Bridge boy, but Lilian never divulged his name.[1]

Propriety was very much a hallmark of the new middle class and subverting that propriety wouldn't have been easy. Girls would normally have been escorted by their brothers. In all probability the liaison happened in a quiet moment at home, when what may have been innocent exploration got out of hand.

Salvation Army hostel, Mare Street, Hackney: purchased by the Salvation Army in 1881 and from 1887 'the Headquarters of the Women's Social Work (informally known as '259') and a training home for women officers'. (The Salvation Army International Heritage Centre, London)

Salem Chapel's Order of Memorial Service for Queen Victoria on 2nd February 1901. The Queen had died on 22nd January. The date was almost exactly nine months before the birth of Lilian's baby. It is wise to assume that coincidence of dates was no more than that. It is tempting nonetheless to think that the suspension of everyday activity associated with Queen Victoria's death may have led to a breakdown of the everyday order, allowing young people accustomed to Wesleyan strictures more than the usual amount of private time together.

The family's understanding today is that Lilian had the opportunity to marry the father but refused to do so. She was determined to go her own way. There would surely have been strong parental pressure to marry. The Spencers were strong Wesleyans, and an illegitimate birth and the stigma attached meant crisis. But a forced marriage may also have been something Lilian's parents couldn't contemplate. The lecture on the sanctity I quote above (see page 19) set a chillingly high bar. If a couple ill-advisedly entered into marriage, the speaker had opined, 'they must submit to the penalty of their folly'.

Salvation

It was through the Salvation Army in Halifax that the London arrangement was made. Their Interview Book records Lilian's case as follows:

'Maternity case. Trouble unknown to parents. Asks if SA can help. Ack Letter 14.2.01. Also wrote 16.2.01. Reply received 19.2.01. Various other letters passed & Colonel inter: girl at Halifax 16.3.01 & agreed to help her. Letter Rec. 20.3 Ans: 23. Mrs B and Col.* Felt it right that she should tell her parents before coming. Mrs Spencer found this letter, & questioned L. then wrote Colonel. Several letters passed. Mrs S saw Mrs Booth in Liverpool April 6th, & arranged that L. should come to Ivy House direct. Arrived 22.4.01.'[2]

Joseph's interest in Home Missions would almost certainly have meant contact, and maybe working with, the Salvation Army in Halifax and other Yorkshire towns. Lilian may have been aware of their work, and how they might possibly help her. To the Army's great credit they avoided moral strictures and put the needs of mother and baby first. But they will, I'm sure, have been well rewarded by Joseph for doing so. Why otherwise arrange for a girl from Hebden Bridge to move to London in April, and live at Ivy House, the hostel where her son was born some five months later? It is possible that Lilian, who we know had shorthand skills, took on work for Ivy House while she was there.

There is a further twist to the story: while living in the Salvation Army's hostel, on Mare Street, London, or through contacts she made while she was there, Lilian met the son of a leading Salvation Army officer, whom she was to marry some five years later.

---

* Mrs B is Florence Booth, the daughter-in-law of the founder of the Salvation Army and the Colonel would have been Adelaide Cox, her second in command. April 6th was Good Friday and they were both in attendance at Hope Hall, Liverpool, 'and seventy seekers sat at the mercy seat on that day'. (Information supplied to Barbara Edwards by Major Kevin Pooley of the Salvation Army.)

A successful cover-up

The Spencers had taken radical measures to cover up the story, and it seems they were successful. There is no evidence to the contrary. To cover their trail they employed a simple fiction: the new arrival was Joseph and Emily's youngest child. Emily had had a boy as late as 1894, and there's a record of a stillborn child in 1899. In 1901 she would have been forty-six. If Lilian did at any point return to Hebden Bridge to see friends it would have been without her son, Geoffrey.

But for the period of the pregnancy neither the real nor the putative mother were living in the town. Friends and local family who knew the story would have been sworn to secrecy. That secrecy was maintained even within the wider family until quite recent times: Geoffrey was 'Uncle Geoff', the youngest of the six boys born to Great-aunt Emily.

25

Taking Refuge

Joseph and Emily would have discussed the options available to them. If Geoffrey was to be their youngest child, Emily would need, assuming they stayed in Hebden Bridge, to keep a low profile, avoid awkward questions, dress as if she was pregnant (maybe not so difficult given the fashions of the time), and then leave town for the later stages of the pregnancy. Lilian would be living away in London, and out of the picture.

The alternative was to avoid subterfuge by moving Emily, and that would mean the whole family, away from Hebden Bridge at an early stage. It seems they took the second course.

Effingham in Surrey would have been the obvious place to move to. Their relations, Edward, one of the two sons who inherited the John Kershaw and Sons business from their father, and his wife, were dead. Their old housekeeper, Harriet, had the house to herself.

Two dates are significant: 23rd March and 1st April. March 23rd is the date of the letter which Emily found among Lilian's belongings. April 1st, nine days later, is the date of the 1901 census and Norman, the eldest of Lilian's four younger brothers, is recorded as staying with Harriet in Effingham. It may or may not have been a planned holiday for Norman: either way it was convenient to have him out of the house at a time of crisis.

At some point it seems that Emily and the other three boys followed him to Effingham. Lilian and Geoffrey would have joined them from Mare Street. The family would then have stayed in Effingham throughout 1902 and the first part of 1903. Joseph would have had plenty of time to plan where the family might live when they moved back up north.

Effingham

Only later in life did Geoffrey talk about the circumstances of his birth. He recalled that for the first years of his life he was brought up by 'a family friend' in Effingham. 'Then when [his] parents began to run out of business and money in Bramhall they took him in as their son.' This would have been in 1906, the year Lilian got married. Up to this point it seems he had been living with Harriet, the 'family friend', and indeed his mother, in Effingham, with

Lilian working nearby as a governess. Shortly after the marriage Lilian and Ernest set off for South Africa, where Ernest already had business interests.

Geoffrey never, to our knowledge, elaborated on his comment about his parents 'beginning to run out of business and money'. But it does open up another dimension to the story, which we will return to shortly.

Barbara Edwards has researched the Effingham link. Edward Kershaw, described as 'a retired draper living on his own means', had died in 1892 and his wife in 1899, 'leaving The Hollies to Harriet, who had been their servant, in a will of which Joseph is the executor. Harriet it was who helped Lilian look after Geoffrey in his infancy'.

We covered the close links, both business and family, between the Kershaws and the Spencers in an earlier chapter. Edward's younger brother, James, was Joseph's employer in his apprentice years. Edward and James were also brothers-in-law to Joseph's father, after Thomas Spencer took Sarah Kershaw as his second wife in 1869. Edward had sold his business to his brother in 1874, though he'd moved south some years earlier.

Effingham and the Pennine cotton towns could not have been more different. Edward swapped the Pennines, moorland, sheep pasture and cotton mills, for rural, wooded and arable Surrey. A Wesleyan link may have helped him fix on Effingham as a possible place to move to (ministers who were obliged never to stay more than two or three years in one place were of necessity widely travelled), and he may have also seen a business opportunity, with the lines of supply he'd built up through his Lancashire business.

Edward would initially have been seen as an outsider, and in 1868, not long after moving to Effingham, he fell out with a group of local men who accused him of mistreating his domestic servant. There was an altercation and Edward was called before the local magistrates to explain his actions. He was found not guilty, but censured. Any local opprobrium seems not to have worried him. He's described in the 1871 census as a master draper, with four visitors, two of whom are drapers from Hebden Bridge.[1]

Not only would Effingham have been a place for the Spencers to escape to for holidays before 1901, it would also have opened their eyes to a very different and slower-paced way of life. Without the option of Effingham Joseph and the family might well have stayed in Hebden Bridge and faced whatever consequences might follow. And it may have influenced Joseph in his choice of Bramhall as a place to settle in 1903.

Effingham and Bramhall were in some senses similar, still largely rural communities with easy access to nearby rapidly expanding conurbations. But Bramhall was on Manchester's doorstep, in open country to the south-east, and yet only a short train ride from the city centre. Stockport and

Macclesfield, with their mill-dominated townscapes, were nearby, and the village of Wilmslow, across the fields from Bramhall, had its own fustian-cutting tradition.

Bramhall

Joseph is not recorded as living in Bramhall on the 1903 electoral roll, but he is there, living at a house called Mayfield, for 1904. The children appear on the roll for the local board school from June 1903.[2] In 1907 Joseph is recorded as residing at Rostrevor in Bramhall. In both cases, even in 1907, 25 Market Street, Hebden Bridge is still listed as the 'qualifying property'. He is recorded as living in Bramhall – but Hebden Bridge is where he would exercise his vote. But not after 1907, when the last link with Hebden Bridge is severed.

The 1911 census has Joseph and Emily living at the house (Endsleigh) they had had built in Bramhall, with Joseph still listed as a ladies' and gents' tailor, and Geoffrey listed not as son, but as grandson, which of course he was, and bearing Lilian's married surname – she had married Ernest Ridsdel in 1906. It seems that the census knew (Joseph couldn't lie to the census) what the wider family and the wider world did not.

Ack Lane, Bramhall, still a village and not yet a leafy suburb, c.1910 looking toward the Victoria Hotel.

Endsleigh was next door to the station, allowing quick access, about thirty minutes, to Manchester London Road (later Piccadilly) Station. It was also a short distance to the local Wesleyan chapel which, like the one in Hebden Bridge, was thriving, with a big congregation, and good middle-class connections. The Spencers would have felt at home, and again it is likely that it was a Wesleyan friend, probably one of the peripatetic ministers who they'd known in Hebden Bridge, who suggested Bramhall as a place where they would feel at home and be well received.

A few years behind Hebden Bridge, but very much in the same spirit, the growing Wesleyan congregation in Bramhall commissioned the building of a new chapel. It was formally consecrated in 1906. The builder was William Lewis Adkinson, who made a very good business developing shops and housing in what is now the modern village. Thomas Spencer and William's daughter, Lily, were the first couple to marry there after its opening.[3]

It is significant that when Lilian married Ernest they chose a local parish church – Church of England – in nearby Woodford. Only a week later her brother, Thomas, married Lily in Bramhall's Wesleyan chapel. The decision to marry in a parish church was obviously a deliberate decision, and remains a mystery.[4]

The wedding of Thomas Spencer and Lily Adkinson, Bramhall Wesleyan Chapel, 1906

Ernest's father was, as we've seen, a senior Salvation Army officer, but it's unlikely that would have influenced their decision either way. Ernest we know from his later life was a man of strong views, and he may have had little sympathy for the mission work so important to both Wesleyan and Salvationists. He may have dictated the decision. Lilian was also, unlike the rest of her family, an outsider in the village of Bramhall. She may have worshipped in the local parish church in Effingham, or in no church at all.

Her personal circumstances would only be known to her family and the bridegroom. It may be that given her previous close association with the Wesleyan chapel in Hebden Bridge she no longer felt comfortable marrying in Wesleyan company, other than her immediate family.

We can imagine the family discussions and probably arguments at the time. Lilian had been the cause of immense disruption. But she had at least come 'home' to Bramhall to get married.

26

Hard Times

The Fustian Weavers' Strike

With branches in Burnley, Accrington and, to the south, in Oldham, and two premises in Manchester, business would have been good for Joseph in the 1890s. Even after the extraordinary domestic disruptions of 1901 there is every reason to assume the business continued to flourish.

Joseph, as we've seen, aspired to be a gentleman's tailor, but fustian (supplying nightwatchman's coats, for example) remained a core part of his business. And for fustian goods the ready supply of fabric would have been essential. For other fabrics he would have brought in supplies from further afield, but for fustian his sources would have been local.

We can assume that the making up of clothes took place primarily on shop premises. But the manufacture of the fustian cloth itself was the work of the mills, and the Fustian Weavers' Strike of 1906–8 may have hit the business hard. The collapse of Joseph's business in 1907 (see below) may have been influenced by a serious interruption of supply:

'As a result of a ballot the weavers at Foster Mill struck, and were followed a week later by 130 employees of Messrs R. Thomas & Son, Hangingroyd Shed ... By early October the strike had reached such proportions that the Rev. A. G. Harding saw fit to preach a sermon on it at Birchcliffe Baptist Church. Everyone was wondering whether it was the beginning of a general strike in the town.'[1]

Joseph had diversified his business in terms of shop premises. But it may have been harder to diversify his sources of supply. 'The weavers, backed by their trade organisations, were insisting on being paid at the same rate as their fellow workers in Bury and other Lancashire towns.' With his local connections he may have been over-reliant on possibly cheaper Hebden Bridge fustian.

'In the trade review for 1906 it was stated that whereas the year had begun well it was ending gloomily, not only as regards fustian weaving but also in the ready-made clothing industry.'

The strike and the crisis which hit Joseph's business in 1907 may or may not have been linked. But there probably was, when Joseph put his business up for sale, a mood of pessimism in the town. The 'entreaties' of the auctioneer recorded in the newspaper reports of the sale of the Market Street property suggest a much higher price had been anticipated.[2]

There's an irony here, though it may be more apparent than real. With no end to the strike in sight a new venture, the Eaves Bottom Self-help Manufacturers Society, was proposed. Inspired by the example of the Fustian Manufacturers Co-operative it would employ striking workers. At the inaugural meeting Councillor Clay, chairman of Hebden Bridge Urban District Council, asserted that 'they were in the midst of a boom that had no precedent in history, and they were glad to see it continue'. Two disused mills were purchased. The new mills 'would weave cotton while the land was intended to be turned into a garden village'.[3]

The *Todmorden & District News* reported wholesale clothiers were looking forward to a busy time. 'There is some complaint about the difficulty of getting cloth.'[4]

Joseph may have read the newspaper reports that August and wondered. But the hard fact was that his Hebden Bridge business was no more – and he had a creditors' meeting coming up the following month.

The strike had as its unlikely headquarters the 'Tin Tab', a Wesleyan chapel originally built as a mission chapel. Only a year before the strike the Wesleyans had opened another, much grander, chapel nearby, at Foster Lane. The chapel, and its twin towers, with their curious top hats in an oriental style (cake decoration or onion also come to mind) testifies to a local community looking forward with faith and confidence in their future. Wesleyan chapels now lay in every direction: Cross Lanes, above and to the west, Walker Lane, high above to the east, Salem, in the heart of the town, and Heptonstall, the original, and the great survivor, looking down from the hill behind. Foster Mill had long had a Wesleyan connection, and the Wesleyans traditionally tried to stay out of politics, as we've seen. How a striking workforce and chapel attendance played out in terms of local loyalties I can't say. And the world after the strike would never be quite the same again. The chapels represented the old certainties, theirs was an age of great preachers, and missions, and self-belief. The year 1910 was the high point for membership of the various branches of Methodism. Foster Lane almost from the moment it was built belonged to another age.

Tin Mission, Wesleyan, the 'Tin Tab', built in 1887. (Jack Uttley)

Foster Lane Wesleyan Chapel, opened 1904. (Jack Uttley)

End of the line

By 1908 the Eaves Bottom venture was already in financial trouble. The strike itself lasted until March 1908. Trade was depressed. But other tailors survived and prospered. This was the decade when Montague Burton and Fifty Shilling Tailors established their chains. Joseph, with distractions elsewhere, may simply have taken his eye off the ball for too long.

Another possibility is that he had borrowed heavily to fund further expansion. This would have left him more exposed in the event of a downturn.

The end when it came had been abrupt.

The *Todmorden & District News* of 10th May 1907 refers to the auctioning ('offering for public competition') of 'two valuable freehold properties in Market Street'. The next sentence is significant. 'There was only a small company present.' It was not a good time to be selling property.

There were two shops, number 25 ('in the occupation of Mr Joseph Spencer and Mr Tomlinson'[5] – a name we've not heard before) and number 26, 'in the occupation of Messrs Altham and Mr Thomas Wheelwright'. Bidding reached £1,750, but 'despite the entreaties of the auctioneer, no further advances could be got'. This does suggest a town where business was suffering and optimism in short supply. Why the two shops had been put on the market at the same time is unclear.

A conveyance of 1907[6] makes specific reference to the sale, and the purchase, by a Mr Young Greenwood:

'By Mr Joseph Spencer of 25 Market Street and 55 Deansgate, Manchester, tailor & draper, to Mr Young Greenwood of Pry, Blackshawhead, farmer, of two shops in Market Street, Hebden Bridge. Transaction also involves William Henry Sutcliffe of Hebden Bridge, solicitor; John William Shaw of Glen Royd, Birchcliffe Road, Hebden Bridge, solicitor. Refers to previous documents. 6 June 1907.'

Young Greenwood may have taken over the business as a going concern, albeit with a different emphasis. There is an October 1910 *Todmorden & District News* advertisement[7] which advises that 'Greenwood and Thomas' of Market Street hold 'a huge stock of every variety of winter coat'. That suggests a focus on bulk purchases – not the way Joseph had advertised his business. The company owning the shop in 1917 is listed in *Kelly's Directory* as 'Greenwood Bros', and I assume is the same company. They are described as a wholesale clothier, and it seems the layout of the premises was not dissimilar to Joseph's time, with 'a second floor cutting room ... whilst on the top floor women joined up pieces of garments using sewing machines ...' (See page 47.)

The final closure came with a creditors' meeting in Manchester in September 1907, reported in the *Todmorden & District News* of 7th September. It gave three current addresses for the business, two in Manchester: 55 Deansgate Arcade (located at 84 Deansgate and probably his office) and St Mary's Parsonage (a street just north of Deansgate, premises he may have used as a warehouse), and 25 Market Street, Hebden Bridge, though this had already been sold at auction. The explanation given by 'the debtor', being Joseph Spencer, is significant: he explained 'certain losses, which he had incurred in respect of sale of the property and leases on shops sold or closed in Burnley, Accrington and Oldham ... more than accounted for the deficiency'.*

Deansgate Arcade, 84 Deansgate, photograph taken July 1900. This is also the address given for Joseph in Slater's Directory of 1903. Arcades were a popular feature in the newly prosperous towns of Lancashire and Yorkshire. Manchester had five, only one of which, Barton Arcade, survives. Deansgate Arcade was demolished in mid-1950s. (Historic England)

It's clear it had been a forced sale on his part and, given no evidence of wider misfortunes in the Lancashire textile industry, and a long history of steady trading, we have to assume an abrupt and unexpected change in circumstance.

But he wasn't bankrupt. The creditors' meeting in 1907 was just that, a meeting of creditors. Joseph's debts were assigned to a trustee, and he and Joseph would have agreed repayment terms. Joseph must have given evidence of an ability to repay the debt, and that suggests that he still had a viable business.

---

* Total claims against the business were £3,097, of which £1,863 were trade creditors, and the assets were 'expected to realise £1,212, leaving a deficit of £1,885'. No one had offered to take the business over, so a deed of assignment was executed with Mr C. Crabtree as trustee, and a committee of inspection representing Messrs W. H. Sykes and Co., Huddersfield, Messrs H. Halliwell and Sons, Halifax, and the Halifax Joint Stock Bank was appointed.

Like so many before and since, Joseph, for reasons about which we can only speculate, couldn't meet the repayments on the substantial mortgages he'd built up over time. He may also have taken on an additional mortgage to build a house in Bramhall. He and his family nonetheless came through the disaster. But thereafter he lived a quieter and much more ordinary life.

A conventional suburban life

The 1911 census lists Joseph as a tailor, as it does his eldest son, Thomas, and also Norman, the oldest of the younger cohort (four boys) of the family, born 1889. Joseph had built a smart family home, Endsleigh, for himself in his new village, and it continued to be the family home until they moved to Essex some years later. Lilian's twins, Olive and William, were born in Bramhall in 1909.

It may also be that in some small degree this exit from his old business had been planned. He was living south-east of Manchester, with an easy train ride from the station, which was almost next door to his house, into Manchester and Deansgate. His eldest son, Thomas, had been managing the Hebden Bridge shop, but he had married in 1906, and would not have wanted to continue working there, even part-time. And finally – it may be that the true story about Lilian's baby had leaked out.

Joseph's exit may have been more abrupt than he would have wished, but he may not have been entirely unhappy with the outcome.

27

Afterlife

Saying goodbye

Joseph maintained his links with the town through the shop until 1907, but close links seems to have ended in 1903 when he retired as a class leader at Salem Chapel. But before that, as an article in the *Todmorden & District News* in February 1902[1] suggests, he remained closely involved with chapel affairs. He did, of course, still have the Birchcliffe Road house at that point. It may be that the family had hoped to return to Hebden Bridge after the baby's birth. At some point Joseph and Emily must have decided that this was impossible and the sale of the house went through in July 1902.

The newspaper article refers to a well-attended Home Missions meeting at the chapel, which Joseph chaired. With its focus on numbers and evangelists and aggressive missionaries and in particular the repetition of the number seven there is something almost apocalyptic about the report.

'The home missionary fund ... supported 89 home missionary ministers ... In addition there were in cities and large towns more than 40 ministers appointed and maintained exclusively by members of the missions or the circuits adjoining. Seven evangelists were at work ... seven district missionaries who devoted themselves to aggressive work in villages and small agricultural towns ...'

It is ironic, as we've mentioned, that it was a Salvation Army not a Wesleyan children's home that gave refuge to Joseph and Emily's daughter when she became pregnant by a local lad in 1901. Also that the husband, Ernest, she married in 1906 was the son of a leading figure in the Salvation Army. He already had southern Africa connections and had little interest in Christian missions, at home or abroad. His activities were entirely commercial.

Joseph had also been involved in a quieter way with the chapel, at a level that never went reported, as a class leader. Classes, to which all members of a particular church or chapel society are allocated, have always been a feature of Wesleyan and Methodist life. A presentation in March 1903 marked the ending of that role for Joseph.

'Last night week a smart affair took place in Salem lecture room, which was specially decorated for the occasion. The members of the Society class led by Mr Joseph Spencer, late of Brentwood House, who has removed his residence from the district, met to do honour to their leader. During the proceedings a beautiful solid silver flower stand was presented to Mr Spencer by Miss Smith on behalf of the class. Spencer suitably acknowledged.'[2]

A silver salver, not a flower stand, with the inscription, 'To Mr Joseph Spencer as a mark of esteem from members of his society class, Salem Wesleyan Church, Hebden Bridge March 12 1903', is still in the family's possession.

Thomas

Thomas is listed as 'Commercial Traveller (for Clothier)' in the 1901 census. It must have been Joseph's intention that Thomas should work in, and maybe take over, the business. When Joseph moved his main business to Manchester, Thomas was put in charge at Hebden Bridge.

A press cutting from 1904[3] suggests that life was not always straightforward for Thomas. The *Todmorden & District News* of Friday 29th July 1904 reports that 'Joseph Spencer, tailor, Hebden-bridge, was summoned for two breaches of the Factory and Workshops Act, viz. i) not reporting overtime, ii) not fixing overtime'. Women were not working to their specified overtime hours and a notice hadn't been appended when it should have been.

What caught my eye was the following: 'Mr Spencer's son had the management of the shop, and on July 14th, being suddenly called away to Manchester, the overtime worked was not reported. The Chairman of the Bench was of the opinion it was only a technical offence, and defendant would be fined 5s in each case.'

I have the sense of an extremely diligent if not officious inspector. Workplace regulation once so terribly lacking had come a long way over the decades.

Endgame

It is important to separate the closure of his Hebden Bridge business from the fortunes of Joseph Spencer himself. He continued after 1907 to live in a comfortable house, one he'd built for himself, in Bramhall, Cheshire. His daughter had married to an ambitious young man who quickly built a fortune for himself and his family. Two of his sons were listed as tailors and we assume working with their father in the 1911 census. And Joseph will surely have retained at the age of fifty-two at least some of the energy and skills that had allowed him to build up his Hebden Bridge business.

He may have remained at his premises at Deansgate Arcade, a popular business address. The outside looks rather grand, the inside less so, with premises opening from corridors which overlooked a central atrium. He may also have retained a small warehouse. His primary business may have been as a middleman, using his business expertise and wide range contacts to link manufacturers, suppliers and retail outlets.

I will let Manchester have a final word. As David Ayerst writes, 'Edwardian Manchester was still in an economic sense something like a city state. The ties [of its merchants] with New Orleans or Alexandria; with Constantinople, Hamburg, Calcutta and Shanghai were in many respects closer than with Birmingham or Newcastle ... A still growing proportion of mankind were clothed from the stately warehouses that lined Portland Street.'

Joseph may have detoured via Portland Street on his walk to work from London Road Station to Deansgate. He had had big ambitions, focused in his case on Burnley or Accrington, rather than Calcutta or Shanghai. They hadn't quite worked out. Heading every day into Manchester may have underlined that disappointment. Maybe when he moved south, to Essex, a few years later, he did so with a sense of quiet relief.

As for Thomas, he continued working as a tailor's representative. He was troubled by serious illness after the war and died young, in 1923, aged just forty-five. But through Thomas and Lily's daughter, Phyllis, her husband, James, and their sons, John and Christopher, the Spencer family retained a link in Bramhall almost to the present day.

Appendix One – Families

1) The family of Joseph and Emily Spencer, as recorded in the family Bible

Joseph Spencer, born in High Street, Hebden Bridge, 30th April 1854; Emily Walton, born at Foster Mill House, Hebden Bridge, 24th July 1855; both of them became members of the Wesleyan Church in 1870; married at Salem Wesleyan Chapel, Hebden Bridge, 29th August 1877.

J. Spencer [this is Joseph] was confirmed at the parish church of Stanford-le-Hope, Essex, by the Bishop of Basildon, on 14th May 1924. [Joseph and Emily had moved to Essex, to a house bought for them by Lilian and her husband. Joseph, it seems, had put Nonconformity behind him.]

Children: Thomas Walton Spencer, born at Salem House, 28th June 1878; Lilian Ethel Spencer, born in Market St, 26th November 1880; Norman Hope Hodgson Spencer, born 25 Market St, 11th April 1889; Charles Wesley Spencer, born at 25 Market St, 9th September 1890; Reginald Stanley Spencer, born at Heath House, 17th August 1892; Robert Hugh Spencer, born at Heath House, 17th April 1894; baby girl (stillborn) at Brentwood, 24th February 1899. [Lilian's son, Geoffrey, was born on 20th September 1901.]

Lilian married E. B. (Ernest) Ridsdel at Woodford Church, Cheshire, 12th May 1906.
Thomas married Lily Adkinson at Bramhall Wesleyan Chapel 16th May 1906. (Thomas died 28th October 1922.)

2) The family of Thomas (senior) and Mary Spencer

Thomas and Mary had five children: Jane Rushton (born 1839, out of wedlock), Hannah (1844), James (1847), Joseph (1854), and Mary Ellen (1858). Hannah and James appear in the 1851 census, and Hannah in the 1861 census, where she is listed as a sewing machinist. Mary Ellen married Virgil Greenwood in 1879.

Mary died in the 1860s and Thomas married Sarah Kershaw, sister of Edward and James Kershaw, in 1869.

APPENDIX ONE – FAMILIES

3) The family of Thomas and Sarah Walton

Thomas and Sarah Walton (married in 1843) had five children: Elizabeth Ann, Sarah Grace, Emily, Robert Spence and Mary Louisa. Emily was born in 1855. She is described in the 1871 census as a cotton winder. Elizabeth Ann, aged twenty-four, is recorded as a milliner, and Sarah Grace also as a milliner, aged nineteen. Robert is fourteen in 1871, and Mary Louisa is eight. (Also living at Foster Mill in 1871 is Thomas's mother, another Sarah, who had married Bannister Halstead in 1841.)

The 1881 census describes Sarah Walton as a widow (Thomas died in 1877) and living at 'Bridge Street, Heptonstall', for which read Market Street, Hebden Bridge. Living with her is daughter Mary (Louisa), described as a draper's assistant – maybe working for Joseph Spencer's business.

Robert Spence Walton is described in the 1891 census as a single man of thirty-four, and a registered medical practitioner, living in Salem Buildings, Calder Place. His mother, Sarah, is living with him in 1891, also his sister, Mary Louisa, still described as a draper's shop assistant.

Mary Louisa, 'late of Robin Hood's Bay, Yorkshire', died, as a spinster, on 22nd December 1950, at a nursing home in Todmorden. She would have been eighty-seven. The author's father, J. B. Collier, as her solicitor, handled probate on her will. The legatees included the family of her sister, Elizabeth Ann, wife of Eli Fielding.

The Walton family gravestone, adjacent to Heptonstall Chapel, it commemorates Thomas Walton (died 1877); Sarah, his wife (died 1891); Sarah, daughter (died 1877, only three months after her father); Robert Spence, son (died 1920); and Mary Louisa, daughter (died 1950).

Appendix Two – a photograph album of family and friends

The album includes photographs of Robert Spence Walton, Emily Spencer's brother, and their much older sister, Elizabeth (Fielding), and her husband, Eli, and their youngest daughter, Beatrice. They appear in the main text, as do photographs of John and Mary Crowther and Tom and Clara Smith, family friends with whom the Spencers shared a close connection at Salem Chapel. For a photograph of the family of Virgil Greenwood, husband of Joseph's younger sister, Mary Ellen, see below.

The appearance of Beatrice Fielding in the album, as a young lady, suggests a date of either side of 1910. It may have been about this time that the Spencers put the album together, although most of the photographs probably date from up to ten years earlier. Beatrice, the youngest of six daughters, was ten in 1901 – a senior student at Hebden Bridge Secondary School in 1908 and listed as an assistant teacher in the 1911 census.

The Greenwood family. Virgil Greenwood was Emily Spencer's brother-in-law. The photo is labelled 'Briercliffe, Burnley', where the Greenwood family lived. I have been unable to make a precise match with the census record so I have not attempted to identify individuals. A photo from several years earlier has the family in almost identical attire. The 1911 census lists the three eldest children as cotton weavers, and the two younger children as part-time school/part-time cotton weavers. It was not until 1918 that the school-leaving age was raised to fourteen, putting an end to part-time work for schoolchildren.

Unidentified photographs. There are a number of unidentified photographs. Two, Wesleyan men of the cloth, are included in the main text. The other photographs are reproduced below. If readers are able to identify any of the individuals involved, please contact the Pennine Horizons archive, which holds copies of all the photographs.

Appendix Three – obituary for Reginald Spencer, printed in the Halifax Courier

REGINALD STANLEY SPENCER
Grove Park (London); formerly of Brentwood (Hebden Bridge)

Rifleman, Queen Victoria's Rifles, killed in action 14 April 1917 listed in volume 76 of the 80 volumes of Soldiers Died [SD] 1914–19

Educated Stubbings Board School, Hebden Bridge & Warehousemen's and Clerks' Schools, Cheadle Hulme. Salem SSch. [Sunday School] Worked for North British & Mercantile Insurance Co. in Manchester.

Enlisted Oct 1914. No 391085. France from Mar 1915. Wounded & shell-shocked Apr 1915. Buried by shell at Loos, prolonged unconsciousness, shell-shock & amnesia in hospital in London.

RTU [returned to unit] Feb 1916, again wounded & shell-shocked Sep 1916. Hospital & convalescent camp until Mar 1917.

Was twice the only survivor in his platoon. Missing NPD [now presumed dead].

Comm[emorated] Arras Memorial. Aged 24.

*

The Book of Remembrance in the new Hebden Bridge Methodist Church lists seventy dead from Foster Lane, Salem and Cross Lane chapels in the two World Wars.

Appendix Four – types of cloth

Fustian

The Wheatsheaf magazine of May 1919, quoted by Tom Greenwood (see Notes for Chapter Three, note 3, above), carried the following description of fustian making:

'Originally it was of linen and cotton; then it became wholly cotton. Corduroy is simply a corded fustian. The stronger kinds of yarn are used in the mill. These are wound and re-wound, to give warps of double, treble or four-fold threads. The threads for the weft also are in the low numbers. They are woven on heavy looms; and, in the case of corduroy, woven so that the weft arches over the strands of the cord – over four and under one, over four and under one. Then the fustian cutter by hand, or by the fashion cutting machine, drives the long rapier-like knives along the threads of the warp, slitting the curves of the arches of the weft. Another process ... serves to turn back the cut weft until the ends on either side of the binding warp are brought together, and intermixed in a pile that will stand up straight and stiff.'

Other cloths

Beaver is 'a double cloth that resembles felted beaver fur, and used for overcoats'.

Kersey is a coarse woollen cloth. 'The yarns were spun ... from inferior carded wool and made thick and sturdy cloth.'

Melton is a woollen cloth, woven in a twill form, with a smooth, felt-like surface, and traditionally used for naval officers' uniforms.

Moleskin is 'a heavy cotton fabric, woven and then sheared to create a short, soft pile on one side to simulate the fur of a mole'.

'Ulstering' is another term which appears in Joseph's advertisements: an ulster was 'a man's long, loose overcoat of rough cloth, typically with a belt at the back'.

*

Worsted wool is spun from combed (as opposed to carded) wool fibre. It has long fibres aligned by the combing process into a smooth, lustrous yarn typically used for tailored items such as suits. Conventional wool has a shorter staple, is much hairier and is typically used for knitted items such as sweaters. See: https://historicaltextiles.com/home/textile-glossary/

Nap refers to 'the raised (fuzzy) surface on certain kinds of cloth, such as velvet or moleskin'.

Shoddy is cloth made from recycled wool and involves grinding woollen rags into a fibrous mass and mixing this with some fresh wool. A similar process involving felt or hard-spun woollen cloth went by the name of mungo. Batley and Dewsbury areas were the centres of production. 'It created a huge demand for rags and waste wool and made clothes much more affordable.'

*

Quotations are from Smith and Monahan (see notes for Chapter Three, note 3), Wikipedia, and the *BBC History Magazine's* History Extra.

Acknowledgements

It was family that led me to Hebden Bridge. But the town quickly took over. I wanted to know what life was like back then, in the late nineteenth century, and how the Spencer family would have experienced it.

Research by members of the family had already opened a few doors, and I'm indebted to my second cousins, Mark Igoe and Barbara Edwards, for their research into the background of their grandmother, and my great aunt, Lilian Spencer. She gives a touch of unexpected drama, and closure, to the story, so my gratitude also goes to Lilian herself.

Another great debt is to members of the Hebden Bridge Local History Society, and to Diana Monahan in particular. She has provided information and charted pathways which I could never have found without her. I'm also indebted to the Pennine Horizons Digital Archive (PHDA), and Ann Kilbey, for not only providing many of the images but also for opening my eyes to what life and landscapes looked like back then. (All images not otherwise referred to here have been supplied by the PHDA.) Also to the Hebden Bridge Local History Archive, to Vin and Susie Bamford, owners of Brentwood, to Michael Peel, Amy Binns, Alan Fowler and Nigel Smith, and to Nigel Smith specifically, for permission to use his map of the townships of the Upper Calder Valley (page 2).

A big thank you to my publisher, Miles Bailey, at The Choir Press, to my editor, Angeline Wilcox, to Terry Ayling, for the map of Hebden Bridge (p. viii) and to my daughter, Rozi, for designing the family tree. Also to my cousin, Kate, who has been the guardian down the years of the family photo album, which has added its own indispensable dimension to the story.

The Jack Uttley Photo Library supplied photographs on pages 33 ,86 and 127. My thanks to John Uttley for his help and guidance. Also to Calderdale Museums and Bridgeman Images for permission to use John Holland's painting of Hebden Bridge. Acknowledgements also to the Frith Collection for photographs on pages 45, 53 and 129, also to the Mary Evans Picture Library (page 75), Woodhouse Grove School (page 116), the Salvation Army Heritage Centre (page 124), Andrew Corrie (page 129), and the Historic England Archive (page 135).

The digitised versions of historic Ordnance Survey mapping are a remarkable resource: my thanks to the National Library of Scotland. Also to the Calderdale Archive, another invaluable resource, for the plans of 25 Market Street (page 47) and Brentwood (page 101).

My bibliography lists a wide range of sources. Two indispensable books have been *History of Hebden Bridge* by Colin Spencer, and *Pennine Valley: A History of Upper Calderdale*, a remarkable collaborative effort edited by Bernard Jennings. For my understanding of the clothing industry I've relied on two books above all others: *The Clothing Industry of Hebden Bridge: Selected Texts*, edited by Nigel Smith and Diana Monahan; and *Mercantile Manchester, Past and Present*, published in Manchester back in 1896, a remarkable picture of the Manchester merchant landscape.

All Our Own Work: The co-operative pioneers of Hebden Bridge and their mill by Andrew Bibby, is superbly researched, and *Valley of a Hundred Chapels* by Amy Binns, is a delight. Several books published by the Hebden Bridge Local History Society have provided in-depth information on specific subjects: one that stands out is *Traditional Food in the Pennines* by Peter Brears.

Last but by no means least I must mention Malcolm Bull's Calderdale Companion website, which he describes as 'a collection of trivia, miscellaneous facts, and some interesting information about Halifax and the Calderdale district ...', which in no way does justice to a quite remarkable resource.

Notes

The following abbreviations are used:

HBLHS: Hebden Bridge Local History Society
TDN: *Todmorden & District News*
TAHBN: *Todmorden Advertiser and Hebden Bridge Newsletter*
HBT: *Hebden Bridge Times*

INTRODUCTION

1. Oscar Handlin and John Burchard (eds.), *The Historian and the City*, the M.I.T. Press, 1963, p. 7.
2. Ted Hughes, *Remains of Elmet*, Faber, 1979.
3. Information supplied by Keith Stansfield.
4. For a booklet, *High Street, Hebden Bridge: the past – and the future*, see http://www.hebdenbridge.co.uk/news/2016/docs/High-Street-Booklet.pdf
5. See Appendix One for more details of the Spencer family.
6. This is confirmed by the fact that when his mother married Bannister Halstead in 1841 (Thomas would have been nineteen) the register shows her to be a spinster. The Halsteads were shuttle-makers, and well known in Hebden Bridge. Bannister would have been a useful connection for Joseph Spencer when setting up his own business.
7. Tom Greenwood, 'The Origins and Development of the Clothing Industry in Hebden Bridge', p. 20. See note 3 under *2. Fustianopolis* (below).

1. THE PENNINE WEAVER

1. E. P. Thompson, *The Making of the English Working Class*, Penguin, 1966, pp. 297–346.
2. Robert Tombs, *The English and their History*, Allen Lane, 2014.
3. Bernard Jennings (ed.), *Pennine Valley: A History of Upper Calderdale*, 1992, reprinted by the Hebden Bridge Local History Society, 2011, pp. 147 and 151.
4. Andrew Bibby, *All Our Own Work: The co-operative pioneers of Hebden Bridge and their mill*, Merlin Press, 2015, p. 15.

2. FUSTIANOPOLIS

1. *The Mills of the Hebden Valley*, Hebden Bridge Alternative Technology Centre, 2011, p. 37.
2. Colin Spencer, *The History of Hebden Bridge*, Hebden Bridge Literary and Scientific Society, 1991, p. 131. For an extended description, see Appendix Four.

³ Nigel Smith and Diana Monahan (eds.), *The Clothing Industry of Hebden Bridge*, HBLHS, 2018. The book contains four unpublished texts. The text quoted here is by S. C. (Sam) Moore, who held a senior position working for the Hebden Bridge Fustian Manufacturing Society. See pp. 92–94. Another text is also directly relevant: Tom Greenwood's 'The Origins and Development of the Clothing Industry in Hebden Bridge'. This is a thesis written in 1982 as part of a Diploma in Labour Studies at Ruskin College, Oxford.
⁴ Stephen Kenny, *Journal of Historical Geography*, January 1982, 'Sub-regional specialisation in the Lancashire cotton industry, 1884–1914'.
⁵ Spencer, p.133.
⁶ Spencer, p. 142.
⁷ See the website, From Fulling to Fustianopolis, http://www.fromfullingtofustianopolis.co.uk, under 'Ready-Made Clothing'.
⁸ From Fulling to Fustianopolis, under 'Trade Directories'.
⁹ *The Mills of the Hebden Valley*, published by the Hebden Bridge Alternative Technology Centre, 2011, pp. 12–27.

3. CATHEDRALS OF NONCONFORMITY

¹ and ² Spencer, op. cit., p. 64.
³ Spencer, p. 59.
⁴ Spencer, p. 69.
⁵ Jennings, p. 130.
⁶ 'The attitude of official Methodism to the world outside' had been as far back as 1820 'exclusively evangelistic'. 'The period from 1830 to 1870 was a period of persistent agitation across society' and 'of the painful and reluctant democratisation of the Methodist constitution.' (Rupert E. Davies, *Methodism*, Penguin, 1963, pp. 140–141.)
⁷ Jennings, p. 134; see also Amy Binns, *Valley of a Hundred Chapels*, Grace Judson Press, Heptonstall, 2013, pp. 53–55.

4. GROWING UP

¹ Bibby, pp. 14–15.
² Jennings, pp. 135–137.
³ Joshua Holden, *A Short History of Todmorden*, Manchester at the University Press, 1912, pp. 197–199.
⁴ Asa Briggs, *Victorian People*, Pelican, 1968, p. 126.
⁵ Spencer, p. 110.
⁶ Jennings, p. 136. Jennings lists the figures for different categories of school in the Todmorden district according to the 1851 census. There were 21 dame schools, 25 private elementary schools and 14 categorised as 'other', 60 in total, and just under 3,000 pupils.
⁷ Jennings, p. 139. The schedule of the local schools prepared in response to the 1870 Act refers to a Wesleyan school at Walker Lane, and not at Salem Chapel.
⁸ E. R. Dickenson, *Salem Wesleyan Church, Hebden Bridge 1824–1924*, Hebden

Bridge, 1924.
9   For the day school at Cross Lanes see Malcolm Bull's Calderdale Companion, for Hollinrake's School see Jennings, p. 138. Henry Hollinrake was also secretary of the Hebden Bridge Co-operative Wholesale Society and is credited with putting their accounts in order after the theft of £600, a vast sum for the times, in 1868.
10 Jennings, p. 139.
11 Source: Georeferenced Maps: https://maps.nls.uk/geo/explore/#zoom=18&lat=53.74281&lon=-2.02377&layers=168&b=1

5. THE WALTONS OF FOSTER MILL

1   Wikipedia, under 'James Walton (inventor)'.
2   *TDN*, 18th July 1909.
3   *TAHBN*, 30th September 1871.
4   *TAHBN*, 13th June 1902.
5   *Todmorden and Hebden Bridge Historical Almanack*, 1897.
6   *TAHBN*, 27th December 1901.
7   *TAHBN*, 21st February 1902.
8   Malcolm Bull's Calderdale Companion and *TAHBN*, 27th December 1901.
9   *TAHBN*, 18th May 1888.
10 http://www.fromfullingtofustianopolis.co.uk/

6. CONNECTIONS

1   *TAHBN*, 4th September 1874.
2   *TDN*, 28th September 1877.

7. SETTING UP SHOP

1   The name Thomas Spencer may have had another resonance for the wider public of the Calder Valley. In August 1783 another of that name had met his end on the scaffold on Beacon Hill above Halifax. Born in Mytholmroyd, he had in an earlier life been an associate of Cragg Vale Coiner David Hartley, who died, also on the scaffold, in York in 1770. Thirteen years later Thomas was a leader of the Halifax Bread Riot, heading a starving crowd which seized a shipment of grain on its way to warehouses in the town. He and a colleague were not spared the rope. 'The hillside ... was white with the upturned faces of the thousands who flocked from the valleys.' See: https://www.hebdenbridge.co.uk/murphys-lore/41.html
2   *TAHBN*, 26th November 1880.
3   Calderdale Archives, ref CMT7/BIP/HB:141 Barker's Terrace runs just north of Market Street, a short distance west of 25 Market Street, where Joseph opened his new shop in 1889.
4   Tom Greenwood, in Smith and Monahan, p. 42.
5   *TDN*, 5th December 1884.

8. TAKING THE TRAIN

1. David N. Taylor, *Hebden Bridge and the Railway in the Nineteenth Century*, Hebden Bridge Local History Society, 2019, p. 20.
2. https://www.timeanddate.com/time/uk/time-zone-background.html
3. Edward Gray, *The Manchester Carriage and Tramways Company*, Manchester Transport Museum Society, 1977. See also Wikipedia.

9. PUTTING DOWN ROOTS

1. HBLHS archive, refs. DD/ROU 21 M: Conveyance, and DD/ROU 22 M: Mortgage.
2. Multiple papers related to the Sutcliffe business are held by the Calderdale Archives. They remain to be investigated but a listing provided by Diana Monahan indicates the wide range of their activities. Property, both business and private, and probate were core activities. Included is the 1880 sale of the Salem Mills Estate, where, on Market Street, Joseph was to open his new premises in 1889.
3. Calderdale Archives, ref. CMT7/BIP/HB:231.
4. http://www.fromfullingtofustianopolis.co.uk/. Also, from the *Todmorden & District News*, 20th January 1882: 'The premises on Bridge Street erected by Messrs J. Hilton and Co., wholesale clothiers,' included 'above the upper storeys … a room running the entire length of the building … down one side runs a table which is 108 feet long and capable of holding close on a hundred machines', which I assume were sewing machines.

10. KNOW YOUR GREENWOODS

1. Malcolm Bull's Calderdale Companion allows a comparison of the popularity of the different surnames in the area. Greenwood was by some margin the most popular.
2. Smith and Monahan, pp. 3–82.
3. Bibby, see also https://1nutclough.wordpress.com/history-2/
4. Bibby, p. 71.
5. *TDN*, 18th January 1878.
6. https://www.briercliffesociety.co.uk/Soldiers.htm
7. See Appendix Three for *Halifax Courier*'s obituary.

11. COTTONOPOLIS

1. Léon Faucher, *Manchester in 1844: Its Present Condition and Future Prospects*, 1844, p. 13.
2. Taylor, p. 31.
3. Faucher, p. 71.
4. Asa Briggs, *Victorian Cities*, Pelican, 1968, p. 93.
5. John Mortimer, *Mercantile Manchester: Past and Present*, Palmer, Howe & Co., 1896, re-published by Plodder Lane Publishing, 2016.

6 John J. Parkinson-Bailey, *Manchester: An Architectural History*, Manchester University Press, 2000, p. 94.
7 Sven Beckert, *Empire of Cotton: A New History of Global Capitalism*, Penguin, 2015
8 Parkinson-Bailey, p. 80.

12. GAME CHANGERS

1 Taylor, p. 61.
2 *Mercantile Manchester*, p. 78.
3 *TAHBN*, 4th January 1884.
4 *TDN*, 10th February 1888.
5 *TDN*, 18th May 1888.
6 *TAHBN*, 3rd October 1890.
7 *TAHBN*, 2nd November 1894.
8 Taylor, p. 57.

13. ALL THE NEWS

1 https://www.britishnewspaperarchive.co.uk/titles/cotton-factory-times
2 *TAHBN*, 23rd February 1894.
3 *TDN*, 16th September 1904.
4 *TDN*, 14th March 1890.
5 *Burnley Express*, 9th January 1895.
6 *TDN*, 27th November 1891 and 1st April 1892. ('The lamplighter ... carried a ladder and a handlamp. He set it up against each lamp, climbed up, turned the cock, and held his handlamp to the mantle. He then repeated his journey in the mornings to shut off each cock again.' Judith Flanders, *The Victorian House*, Harper Perennial, 2004, p. 353.)
7 *TAHBN*, 28th December (rejection) and 1st February 1895 (plan passed).
8 *TAHBN*, 30th June 1893.

14. EPIDEMIC

1 Stefan Muthesius, *The English Terraced House*, Yale University Press, 1964, pp. 34, 35.
2 Muthesius, pp. 117, 121.
3 Work on the new sewage works for Todmorden had begun at Sandbed (Charlestown), 'on the site of St James cricket field', in 1901. Seven years passed before it was formally opened in 1908.

15. HOME AFFAIRS

1 *TAHBN*, 3rd January 1890.
2 *Halifax Courier*, 27th September 1862.
3 *TAHBN*, 31st August 1893.
4 *HBT*, 7th January 1898.
5 *Halifax Courier*, 21st November 1896.

6 Footlight Notes, https://footlightnotes.wordpress.com/tag/milton-ray/
7 *TAHBN*, 5th May 1882.
8 *TAHBN*, 27th April 1888.
9 Brass bands would be leading the way. They were part of the non-conformist landscape, and as popular with factory owners as with their workers. Competitions were a popular entertainment, but not one Saturday in late May 1885. The Hebden Bridge Brass Band were the organisers, the venue a field in Mytholm. 'The weather during the forenoon was exceedingly wet, and the temperature was more like that of February then of May.' Ten of the thirteen bands played the same piece, 'Worthy is the lamb', from Handel's Messiah'. A set of waltzes had also been planned but the bad weather saw to that. (TAHBN 22nd May 1885).

16. CHAPEL AND CHOIR

1 Dickenson, p. 19.
2 *Todmorden and Hebden Bridge Almanack* for 1867: 'Scottish Union agents Thomas Walton and James Kershaw … Albert Chambers, [Hebden Bridge], also agent for The National Boiler Insurance Co.' Research by Michael Peel and Diana Monahan. HBLHS archive reference: THB1 1867 to 1871.
3 Spencer, p. 143.
4 *TDN*, 18th February 1898.
5 Jennings, p. 134.
6 Reported in the obituary of Mr J. Blackburn, *TDN*, 17th June 1898.
7 Talk given by David Baker to the HBLHS, 22nd January 2019.
8 *TAHBN*, 3rd August 1877.

17. GOOD WORKS

1 *TAHBN*, 2nd January 1874.
2 *TDN*, 28th December 1888.
3 *TDN*, 3rd January 1890.
4 *TAHBN*, 21st September 1888.
5 *TDN*, 22nd June 1888.
6 *TDN*, 24th October 1890.
7 *TDN*, 5th April 1895.
8 F. C. Pritchard, *The Story of Woodhouse Grove School*, 1978, p. 58; Nigel Watson, *Χαίρετε, Woodhouse Grove: The First 200 Years*, 2011.
9 My Wesleyan Methodists website: https://www.mywesleyanmethodists.org.uk
10 My Wesleyan Methodists website: https://www.mywesleyanmethodists.org.uk
11 Lilian Lewis Shiman, 'The Band of Hope Movement, Respectable Education for Working-Class Children', *Victorian Studies*, vol. 17, Indiana University Press, 1973.
12 Briggs, *Victorian People*, p. 140.
13 Malcolm Bull's Calderdale Companion.

18. RELAXING

1. Jennings, p. 134.
2. Bibby, p. 85.
3. *TAHBN*, 3rd August 1877.
4. *TAHBN*, 7th June 1889.
5. Frank Beckwith, *Yorkshire Historical Fiction*, Dalesman, 1947.
6. https://www.english-heritage.org.uk/visit/inspire-me/blog/blog-posts/history-of-lighting/ See also Judith Flanders, *The Victorian House*, Harper Perennial, 2003, p. 170.

19. THE WIDER WORLD

1. Jennings, p. 134.
2. Thompson, p. 819.
3. Bibby, pp. 19–21.
4. Bibby, p. 93.
5. Bibby, p. 89.
6. Davies, p. 140.
7. Briggs, *Victorian Cities*, p. 123.
8. Thompson, p. 385.
9. Thompson, p. 45.
10. David Ayerst, *Guardian: Biography of a Newspaper*, Collins, 1971, p. 278.
11. Jennings, p. 154.

20. MOVING HOUSE

1. Spencer, p. 20.
2. Calderdale Archive reference: CMT7/BIP/HB:348.
3. Muthesius, p. 31.
4. Muthesius, p. 40.
5. Muthesius, p. 237.
6. Muthesius, p. 244.
7. For J. Hepworth & Son see p. 120.
8. Muthesius, p. 236.
9. Nikolaus Pevsner, *Yorkshire: The West Riding*, in *The Buildings of England* series, second edition, 1967, p. 229.
10. Compare Muthesius, p. 14.

21. FROM TOWNSHIP TO TOWN

1. Spencer, p. 82, and Holden, p. 208.
2. *Halifax Journal*, 1st August 1839. 'On Monday last the peaceable little town of Hebden Bridge (which adjoins the line of the Manchester and Leeds railway now forming) was thrown into the greatest the state of alarm by a number of the excavators from the works of Messrs Moss and Taylor running through the town in the wildest confusion and disorder, pursued by about double their

number of railwaymen, armed with pick-shafts, picks, shovels, &c. ... These latter were English, who had united to drive all the Irish from the line; they then drove them completely out of the town, and went about in a large body to the different public houses searching the rooms, vowing and swearing death to any Irishman they should find.'

3 'City in the Hills: Dawson City and the building of the Walshaw Dean Reservoirs' – talk given by Corinne McDonald and Ann Kilbey, HBLHS, December 2012.
4 Spencer, p. 88.
5 Hebden Bridge Local History Society newsletter, February 2021.
6 There's a family tradition of banking with the District Bank which continues indirectly to this day. NatWest took over the District Bank in the 1970s.
7 *Kelly's Directory* for the West Riding of Yorkshire, 1901.
8 *TAHBN*, August 3rd 1877.
9 Briggs, *Victorian Cities*, p. 109.
10 Malcolm Bull's Calderdale Companion.

22. THE SPENCER CHILDREN

1 'From Weaver to Web,' https://www.calderdale.gov.uk/wtw/search/controlservlet?PageId=Detail&DocId=102378
2 https://histclo.com/style/skirted/kilt/usage/ku-c19.html
3 Spencer, p. 93.
4 Jennings, p. 139.
5 Spencer, p. 97.
6 Spencer, p. 97.
7 Watson, p. 13.
8 Watson, p. 25.
9 Pritchard, p. 213.
10 Watson, p. 52.
11 Watson, p. 110.
12 See https://oumnh.ox.ac.uk/great-debate
13 *The Youth's Instructor and Guardian*, J. Mason (pub.), 1854.
14 Agnes Giberne, *Sun, Moon and Stars*, Seeley and Co., 1891.
15 See https://cplhs.files.wordpress.com/2015/09/peninsula-schools.pdf
16 *TDN*, 5th August 1898, awarded 'second-class elementary' in a shorthand examination, along with her neighbour Lillie Pickles.
17 'Building Our Past: The History of Everyday Buildings,' see https://buildingourpast.com/category/fashion-and-clothing/page/2/

23. AN ABRUPT DEPARTURE

1 HBLHS archive, res. DD/ROU 35 S: Letter and DD/ROU 36 M: Mortgage.
2 *TAHBN*, 22nd August 1902.
3 See a marriage announcement in *TDN*, 11th August 1905.
4 Smith and Monahan, p. 45.

24. FAMILY SCANDAL

1. Lilian never divulged his identity but late in life, when telling the story to one of her granddaughters, she mentioned that his surname was Pickles, a popular surname in the Upper Calder Valley.
2. Ivy House on Mare Street, Hackney, had been opened in 1890 by the Salvation Army as 'a maternity and rescue home'. In May 1894 'the rescue work was moved to a different site and Ivy House became the Salvation Army's first dedicated maternity hospital'. (From Salvation Army records held at https://archiveshub.jisc.ac.uk/ Jisc Archives hub.)

25. TAKING REFUGE

1. Journal of the Effingham Local History Society.
2. Family Search, 'England, Cheshire, School Records, 1796–1950'.
3. Andrew Corrie, *An Illustrated History of Methodism in Bramhall*, 1971.
4. 'A Manchester newspaper at that time [it would have been 1901] describing the suburb of Bramhall concluded with the remark that anyone going to reside there had better become a Wesleyan as that body was so strong in the village.' Quoted in a souvenir handbook from 1955, marking fifty years since the building of the new chapel.

26. HARD TIMES

1. Hebden Bridge Literary & Scientific Society: Local history booklet Vol 3, 'The fustian weavers strike at Hebden Bridge 1906-1908.
2. *TDN*, 19th May 1907.
3. *TAHBN*, 16th August 1907.
4. *TDN*, 30th August 1907.
5. There is an 1897 conveyance of the Hole in the Wall Inn which refers to a Messrs Tomlinson and Greenwood, and a Walter Tomlinson is living at Old Gate according to the 1911 census. Otherwise we have little to go on as to whom his associate might be. (Research by Diana Monahan.)
6. HBLHS archive ref. DD/ROU 42 M: Conveyance.
7. *TDN*, 14th October 1910.

27. AFTERLIFE

1. *TDN*, 7th February 1902.
2. *TAHBN*, 20th March 1903.
3. *TAHBN*, 29th July 1904.

Bibliography

Beesley, Ian, *Through the Mill: The Story of Yorkshire Wool in Photographs*, Dalesman Books, 1987

Bibby, Andrew, *All Our Own Work: The co-operative pioneers of Hebden Bridge and their mill*, Merlin Press, 2016

Binns, Amy, *Valley of a Hundred Chapels*, Grace Judson Press, Heptonstall, 2013

Briggs, Asa, *Victorian Cities*, Pelican Books, 1968

Briggs, Asa, *Victorian People*, Pelican Books, 1965

Chambers, James, *The English House*, Methuen, 1986

Corrie, Andrew, Methodism in Bramhall, third edition, 2021

Davies, Rupert E., *Methodism*, Penguin Books, 1963

Dickenson, E. R., *Salem Wesleyan Church, Hebden Bridge 1824–1924*, Hebden Bridge, 1924

Dyos, H. J., and Wolff, Michael, *The Victorian City: Images and Realities, Volume I Past and Present/Numbers of People*, paperback, Routledge and Kegan Paul, 1976

Dyos, H. J., and Wolff, Michael, *The Victorian City: Images and Realities, Volume II Shapes on the Ground/A Change of Accent*, Routledge and Kegan Paul, 1978

Faucher, Léon, *Manchester in 1844: Its Present Condition and Future Prospects*, Simpkin Marshall, 1844

Flanders, Judith, *The Victorian House*, Harper Perennial, 2004

Fustianopolis – Hebden Bridge: the growth of a textile town, Hebden Bridge Alternative Technology Centre, 2011

Giles, Colum, and Goodall, Ian H., *Yorkshire Textile Mills 1770--1930*, HMSO, 1992

Girouard, Mark, *Life in the English Country House*, Yale University Press, 1978

Gorman, John, *To Build Jerusalem: A Photographic Remembrance of British Working-Class Life 1875–1950*, Scorpion Publications, London, 1980

Handlin, Oscar, and Burchard, John, (eds.), *The Historian and the City*, the M.I.T. Press, 1963

Harker, Margaret, *The Linked Ring: The Secession Movement in Photography in Britain*, 1892–1910, Heinemann, 1979

Hobsbawm, E. J., *The Pelican Economic History of England, Volume 3, From 1750 to the Present Day*, Pelican Books, 1969

Hughes, Ted, (poems), and Godwin, Fay, (photographs), *Remains of Elmet*,

Faber and Faber, 1979

Jennings, Bernard, (ed.), *Pennine Valley, A History of Upper Calderdale*, Hebden Bridge WEA Local History Group, 1992

Longmate, Norman, *The Hungry Mills: The Story of the Lancashire Cotton Famine 1861–65*, Maurice Temple Smith, 1978

Mortimer, John, *Mercantile Manchester: Past and Present*, Manchester, Palmer, Howe & Co., 1896

Muthesius, Stefan, *The English Terraced House*, Yale University Press, 1982

Old Ordnance Survey Maps: Hebden Bridge 1905, reprinted/published by Alan Godfrey Maps, Consett, 1997

Parkinson-Bailey, John J., *Manchester: An Architectural History*, Manchester University Press, 2000

Pevsner, Nikolaus, *The Buildings of England, South Lancashire*, Penguin Books, 1969

Pevsner, Nikolaus, *The Buildings of England, Yorkshire West Riding, second edition*, Penguin Books, 1967

Pritchard, F. C., *The Story of Woodhouse Grove School*, published by Woodhouse Grove School, Apperley Bridge, 1978

Smith, Nigel, and Monahan, Diana, (eds.), *The Clothing Industry of Hebden Bridge, Selected Texts*, HBLHS, 2018

Spencer, Colin, (text), Monahan, Diana, (ed.), *A Century of Change: 100 Years of Hebden Bridge and District*, Hebden Bridge Literary and Scientific Society, 1999

Spencer, Colin, *The History of Hebden Bridge*, Hebden Bridge Literary and Scientific Society, 1991

Taylor, David N., *Hebden Bridge and the Railway in the Nineteenth Century*, Hebden Bridge Local History Society, 2019

The Mills of the Hebden Valley, Hebden Bridge Alternative Technology Centre, 2011

Thompson, E. P., *The Making of the English Working Class*, Penguin, Books, 1966

Watson, Nigel, *Χαίρετε, Woodhouse Grove: The First 200 Years*, Jeremy Mills Publishing Ltd, 2011

Among the websites consulted were:

Malcolm Bull's Calderdale Companion is an indispensable source: http://www.calderdalecompanion.co.uk

http://www.fromfullingtofustianopolis.co.uk/

https://historicengland.org.uk/images-books/publications/textile-mills-lancashire-legacy/textile-mills-lancashire-legacy/

https://en.wikipedia.org/wiki/History_of_cotton

http://www.hebdenbridge.co.uk/history
https://en.wikipedia.org/wiki/Fustian
https://www.themeister.co.uk/birchall/fustian_cutting.htm
https://www.calderdale.gov.uk/wtw/index.html
https://buildingourpast.com/category/fashion-and-clothing/page/2/ (Building Our Past: The History of Everyday Buildings)
http://www.hebdenbridge.co.uk/news/2016/docs/High-Street-Booklet.pdf for the online booklet High Street, Hebden Bridge: the past – and the future
http://www.andrewalston.co.uk/cottonindustryjobs.html
https://www.youtube.com/watch?v=lYocLfZbCeA (for Heptonstall Chapel, opened in 1764, and the 'mother chapel' of Salem Chapel in Hebden Bridge) as featured in the BBC Four series, *Churches: How to Read Them*, by Dr Richard Taylor

Index

Adkinson, William Lewis, 130
Aladdin, 74
American Civil War, 54
Anti-Corn Law League, 94

bazaar (sale of work), 31, 70–71
Buildings Act, 1848, 65
Briggs, Asa, 94
'Briggs of Bristol', 56
Band of Hope, 19, 85–86
Baptists, 16–18, 24, 78, 80–81, 88–89, 94
Barker, William, 12–13, 34, 60
Bibby, Andrew, *All Our Own Work*, 8
Birchcliffe Chapel, 78, 80
Birchcliffe Road, 63–64, 77, 95, 98–101, 108, 110, 121–23, 134, 137
Black Pit Holme, 45, 97
board schools, 24, 111, 115, 129, 144
Boer War, 31, 95
Bramhall, 127–31, 136, 138–40
brass band(s), 23, 31, 73, 76, 154
Brears, Peter, *Traditional Food in the South Pennines*, 102
Brentwood, 100–103, 121–22, 138, 140, 144
Bridge Lanes, 3, 25, 39, 67
Bridge Mill, 14
Briercliffe, 51, 142
'British' schools, 22
Brunswick Terrace, 65, 70, 97
Burnley, 35, 42, 44, 48, 51, 60, 63, 132, 135, 139, 142, 153
  Joseph Spencer's shop, 63

Calder Valley, 2, 8, 10, 42, 71, 100, 102, 147, 151
Calderdale Archives, 38, 46, 151–52
Carlyle, Thomas, 52
census, 2–4, 11–13, 17–18, 21, 28, 34, 37–38, 51, 57, 100–101, 103, 119, 127–29, 136, 138, 140–42
Chadwick, Edwin, 68
church choirs, 79–80
cholera, 68
Church Commissioners, 18
Church of England, 16, 18, 22, 84, 115, 130

cinematograph/theatograph, 74
Combination Acts, 1799, 1800, 7
Commercial Hotel, Hebden Bridge, 46
corduroy, 5, 10, 48, 145
Cotton Factory Times, 62
Cottonopolis, 52
cotton mill(s), 4, 11, 14, 28, 32–33, 67
Cragg Vale Chapel, 85
creditors' meeting, 1907, 133, 135
Cross Lanes Chapel, 17, 23, 138
Crowther, John, 12, 31, 34, 36–37

Deansgate, Manchester 55, 134–36, 139
Doghouse chapel, Todmorden, 22
dual economy, 104

Eaves Bottom Self-Help Manufacturers Society, 133–34
Ebenezer Chapel, 17
Education Act, 1870, 24, 95, 114
1902, 95
Edwards, Barbara, 88, 119, 128, 147
Effingham, 34, 127–28, 131

Fielding, Eli, 31, 34, 36–37, 45, 68, 78–79, 123, 141
  enteric fever (typhoid), 66
Factory Act, 1833, 22
  1844, 21–22
Factory and Workshops Act, 138
Faucher, Léon, *Manchester in 1844: Its Present Condition and Future Prospects*, 52
Fielden Brothers, 54
Fielden, John, 7–8
fire brigade, 31–33, 60
Foster Mill, 4, 23, 28–30, 32–33, 60, 65, 67, 106, 132–33, 140–41
  fire, 14, 32–33, 60
fustian, 1, 9–15, 34–35, 48–49, 55, 104, 132, 145
Fustian Co-operative Manufacturing Society (Nutclough), 11, 13, 49, 51, 94, 96
fustian cutter, 3, 34, 49, 145

fustian cutting, 4, 9–12, 15, 129
Fustian Weavers' Strike, 132
Fustianopolis, 10
fustians, 10–11, 49, 55–56

Giberne, Agnes, *Sun, Moon and Stars*, 118
glees and glee clubs, 81, 92
Greenwood, James, 49
Greenwood, John, of Slack, 46, 49
Greenwood, Joseph, 8, 21, 31, 49–50, 68, 89, 92–93, 96
Greenwood, Virgil, 49–50, 63, 140, 142
  Mary Ellen, 3, 9, 49, 140, 142
Greenwood, Young, 49, 134

half-day Saturday, 4
half-timers, 22, 24, 89
Halifax Courier, 29, 73–74, 82, 106, 144
Halstead, Bannister, 38, 141, 149
  Handel, 38, 68
handloom weavers, 1, 6–7, 11, 16
Hangingroyd Mill, 13–14, 36, 122, 132
Hartley, John (dialect author), 90
Heath House, 36, 39, 70, 97–98, 102, 140
Hebden Bridge
  Agricultural Show, 73
  Co-op, 74, 81, 85, 89–93, 102, 107, 109, 151
  Commercial Association, 61
  District Board, 106
  Gas Company, 29, 91
  Highway and Nuisance Committee, 63
  Building and Nuisance Committee, 99
  Joint Stock Company, 107
  Local Board, 30, 34, 63, 68, 104
  Nuisance Inspector, 64
  Sanitary District, 69
  School Board, 36
  Urban District Council, 106, 133
Hebden Bridge Station, 42, 58
Hebden Bridge Times, 35, 60, 62, 90–91, 107, 149
Heptonstall, 2–4, 7–8, 15–16, 23–24, 30–31, 73, 85–86, 89, 104, 113, 133, 141, 150, 158, 160
Hepworth, J. and Son, 99, 120
High Street, 3, 8, 25, 34, 55, 97–98, 140, 149, 160
History of Typhus in Heptonstall Slack, 7
Hodgson, Sarah, 4, 140

Holden, Joshua, *A Short History of Todmorden*, 104
Hole in the Wall (pub), 85–86, 157
Holmes, J. P., 13
Hope Chapel, 17, 107
Hudson Shaw, Rev. G. W., 93
Huxley and Wilberforce, debating Darwin, 117

India, 54, 85
Irish labourers, 104, 155–56

Kelly's Directory, 13, 49, 108, 110, 134, 156
Kershaw, Edward, 34, 41, 127–28, 140
Kershaw, James, 34, 36, 78–79, 140, 154
Kershaw, John, and Sons, 12, 34–35, 40, 62, 127
Kershaw, Sarah, second wife of Thomas Spencer, senior, 28, 128, 140

ladies' boarding and day school, 119
Lancashire and Cheshire Telephone Company, 60
Lancashire and Yorkshire Railway, 12, 42, 52, 56, 58, 61
Lancashire cotton towns, 5, 42, 104
lending libraries, 89–90, 91
lending libraries (Sunday school), 19, 89
Liberal Club, 31, 89, 95

Manchester, 10–15, 35–36, 39–42, 44, 52–57, 59–62, 85, 95–96, 104, 108, 128, 130, 132, 134–36, 138–39, 144
  warehouses, 55–57
Manchester and Leeds Railway, 42, 104
Manchester and Liverpool District Bank, 57, 108
Manchester Carriage Company, 44
Manchester Evening News, 39
Manchester Guardian, 95, 96, 118, 155–56
'Manchester trade', 11, 55
Mare Street, Hackney, 127
Market Street, Hebden Bridge, 3, 25, 31, 38, 40, 42, 45–46, 49, 60, 65, 70, 76, 97, 100, 107–108, 121, 132, 135
Market Street, no. 25, 46, 47, 129, 134–35
Market Street, Manchester, 42, 53
marriage, 4, 21, 25, 68, 128, 130, 140, 156
  connections by, 9, 28, 68
  sanctity of, 16, 19–20, 125

INDEX

maypole dancing, 112
Mechanics' Institute, 92–93, 96
Mercantile Manchester, 44, 52, 55–56, 59, 152
Methodists, 6, 19, 84
midden privies, 66, 69
Millstone Grit, 10
moleskin, 10, 48, 146
Moore, Sam 11–12
More, Hannah, 22
mortgage, 37, 45–46, 99–100, 110, 121–22, 134, 136
Moss Brothers, 13, 45, 122
Mrs Beeton's Book of Household Management, 102
Mytholm, 18, 36, 70, 97, 114, 154
Mytholmroyd, 1, 8, 33, 66, 151

'National' school, 114
Nonconformist, 28, 80–81, 85, 92, 114
nonconformity, 16, 19, 22, 140
novels for older children, 88
Nutclough Mill, 13, 49, 50, 94, 96, 105

Old Gate, 60, 85, 157
   traffic, 106
Oxford University, 93, 117–18

Pace-egg plays, 112–13
Peel, Michael, 12
Pevsner, Nikolaus, 100
Pickles, George, 32, 83
Poor Law, 8, 73
   Amendment Act, 8
   Guardians (Todmorden), 39
Portland Street, Manchester, 55, 139
power looms, 7

Queen Victoria's Diamond Jubilee, 24, 85

reading and writing skills, 21–22
Redman Brothers, 33
refreshment rooms, 108
Regent Works, 122
Ridsdel, Ernest, 128–131, 137, 140
Rochdale Canal, 42
Royal Exchange, Manchester, 53, 59

Salem Chapel, 17, 19, 23, 29, 31, 34, 36, 56, 70–73, 77, 79, 82–84, 87–88, 103, 112, 114, 137, 142
ministers, 77, 103
   new chapel, 70, 79, 84
   new manse, 78
   new organ, 83
   Sunday school, 17, 22–23, 70, 78, 82–84, 114–15
   missions, home and overseas, 73, 83–85, 125, 137
Salem Mill, 25
Salvation Army, 124–25, 131, 137, 147, 157
Sanger's Circus, 75
school boards, 95, 114
sewing class, 72, 82
Shaw, John, 103, 122
signing the pledge, 86
Smith, Benjamin, 13
Smith, Tom, 57, 78–80, 88, 103
snob row, 99, 101, 122
solicitors, 45, 110, 122, 134
Spencer, Colin, 13, 79, 148–149
Spencer, Charles Wesley, 111, 113, 140
Spencer, Emily, 4, 16–17, 21–25, 28, 30–31, 37–38, 45, 63, 70–74, 80, 85–88, 94, 98, 102, 106, 108, 111, 114–15, 118–19, 121, 124–27, 129, 137, 140–42
Spencer, Geoffrey, 124, 126–29, 140
Spencer, Joseph, 1, 3–5, 8–9, 11–13, 15–17, 21–25, 28, 31–42, 44–46, 48–52, 54–58, 60–64, 68, 70–74, 76–80, 82–100, 103–11, 113–17, 119–23, 125–29, 132–42
   family connections, 34, 70, 103, 142
   education (Joseph and Emily), 22–24
   class leader at Salem Chapel, 137
Spencer, Lilian, 19, 32, 38, 88, 103, 111, 113–15, 118–20, 124–31, 136, 140, 147, 157
   education, 119–20
   pregnancy, 124–26
Spencer, Norman, 111, 127, 136, 140, 159
Spencer, Reginald, 51, 111, 113, 140, 144
Spencer, Robert, 111, 140
Spencer, Thomas, father of Joseph, 11
Spencer, Thomas, son of Joseph, 3–4, 11, 21, 28–30–32, 34, 38, 50, 52, 60, 63, 71, 73, 77–78, 83, 88, 90, 94–95, 106, 111, 113–22, 128, 130, 136, 138–41, 149, 151, 154
   education, 115–118

managing shop, 138
Spencer, Thomas (Halifax Bread Riot, 1783), 151
Spencer, Zechariah, 3
Spencers, Jane and Hannah, 12
St George's Bridge, 106
St George's Square, 49, 99, 112
St James the Great, Hebden Bridge, 17
Stiles, Samuel, *Self-help*, 22, 85, 133
street lighting, 106
Schools (Hebden Bridge),
   Stubbings, 24, 98, 115, 144
   Central, 98, 115
Sunday schools,19, 21–24, 84, 89
Sutcliffe, John, 101
Sutcliffe, William Henry, 45–46, 110, 134

tableaux vivants, 72
telephone, 58–60, 74
'Telephonic Exchange', 59
ten-hour day, 4
The Croft, Hebden Bridge, 107
Theatre Royal, Halifax, 74
Thompson, E. P., *The Making of the English Working Class*, 6–7, 94
Tin Tab, 133
Todmorden, 7–8, 11, 17–19, 21–23, 29, 32, 39, 42, 46, 54, 60, 62, 66, 68, 70, 72–73, 75, 81, 83– 85, 89–90, 93, 99, 104, 114, 141
   library, 89–90
   Industrial Co-operative Society, 89, 93
   District School Board, 114
   (Poor Law) Guardians, 39
Tombs, Robert, *The English and their History*, 6

top and bottom houses, 50, 66, 97
Tyrolean (bazaar and choir), 70–71, 80

Victoria Station, Manchester, 42, 44, 52, 55–r56

Wadsworth, 2, 8, 104
Walker Lane Chapel, 23
Walshaw Dean reservoir, 30
Walton, Dr (Robert) Spence, 4, 28, 30–31, 141–142
   Prince George Masonic Lodge, 32
Walton, Thomas, 4, 16, 21–23, 28–32, 38, 78, 90, 96, 106, 140–42, 151, 154
Wesley, Charles, 79
Wesley, John, 21, 79, 84, 115
   A Plain Account of Christian Perfection, 84
Wesleyan Methodists, 4, 16, 18, 94, 154
Wesleyan
   annual dole of linen goods, 73, 82
   Female Sewing Class, 82
   Million Guinea Challenge, 85
   Mutual Improvement Society, 19
   West London Mission, 84
wholesale clothiers, 12–13, 34, 36, 49, 61, 99, 133–34, 152
Widdop reservoir, 106
Women's Co-operative League, 90
Woodford, 130, 140
Woodhouse Grove School, 115–16, 154
working-class housing, 65, 101
worsted, 48, 55, 146

Youth's Instructor and Guardian, The, 118